THE ECONOMICS OF ENERGY SELF-SUFFICIENCY

Eileen Marshall
and
Colin Robinson

British Institutes' Joint Energy Policy Programme
Policy Studies Institute
Royal Institute of International Affairs

THE ECONOMICS OF ENERGY SELF-SUFFICIENCY

**Eileen Marshall
and
Colin Robinson**

 Heinemann Educational Books

Heinemann Educational Books Ltd,
22 Bedford Square, London WC1B 3HH
LONDON EDINBURGH MELBOURNE AUCKLAND
HONG KONG SINGAPORE KUALA LUMPUR NEW DELHI
IBADAN NAIROBI JOHANNESBURG PORTSMOUTH (NB)
KINGSTON PORT OF SPAIN

First published 1984
ISBN 0 435 84518 7

Printed in Great Britain by
Paradigm Print, Gateshead, Tyne & Wear

CONTENTS

v

TABLES

FOREWORD

In 1982 the British Institutes' Joint Energy
Policy Programme (BIJEPP) embarked on a study of
an energy self-sufficiency policy for the United
Kingdom. Belief in the virtues of self-
sufficiency is often implicit in statements about
energy policy, but rarely is there any explicit
analysis of the feasibility and desirability of
prolonging self-sufficiency in the United Kingdom
(which at present is a net exporter of energy).
A series of BIJEPP papers, listed on the back
cover, explains the results of the work. Most of
these papers discuss self-sufficiency from the
standpoint of a particular fuel (coal, oil, gas or
electricity) and another considers energy
conservation. In this volume, however, we take a
more general overview of the economics of energy
self-sufficiency in the United Kingdom, drawing on
some material from the other papers. Our purpose
is partly descriptive: in Chapters 1 and 2 we show
how, in terms of self-sufficiency, the United
Kingdom energy market has changed in the past and
how governments have seen self-sufficiency as a
policy aim. In Chapter 3, we discuss how the
energy self-sufficiency ratio may change, on the
assumption of unaltered government policy. Then,
in the remaining chapters, we turn to analysis and
prescription, examining various approaches to a
self-sufficiency policy and why it might seem
desirable - for example, because it might improve
the security of fuel supplies, keep down prices in
the long run, bring macro-economic advantages or
confer benefits on future generations.
We conclude that these objectives would more
likely be achieved by maintaining a judicious mix
of imports and home supplies well into next
century rather than by aiming at self-sufficiency.

ACKNOWLEDGEMENTS

We are indebted to George Ray and John Pinder for helpful
comments on a draft of this paper; to Liz Blakeway for
dealing with several drafts and producing the final version
with her usual skill and speed; and to Jackie Reed who
prepared Figure 1. Responsibility for the contents rests,
of course, with the authors.

Chapter One

A HISTORICAL REVIEW OF UK ENERGY PRODUCTION AND CONSUMPTION TRENDS

This introductory chapter reviews trends in energy production, consumption and self-sufficiency in the United Kingdom. Our survey concentrates on the period since the Second World War (though making comparisons with the earlier years of this century), using as a statistical basis Tables 1.1 to 1.4 and Figure 1.1.

The statistics

Tables 1.1 and 1.2 give statistics for energy production and consumption for selected years back to 1923. Although it is not possible to be sure that prewar statistics are in all cases precisely comparable with those for the postwar years, comparability is sufficiently close for the tables to provide a good indication of trends over the period considered. The unit of measurement is million tonnes coal equivalent (mtce).

Consumption statistics are divided into energy uses and non-energy uses; the second category includes, for example, petroleum used as lubricants, bitumen and chemical feedstock. Supplies of fuel for marine bunkers used in foreign (not coastal) trade are also shown separately. Since, as explained in the Foreword, there is considerable confusion over the term 'self-sufficiency' we adopt an explicit definition for the purposes of this chapter. The self-sufficiency ratio, which is given at the foot of Table 1.1 and Table 1.2, is the ratio of UK home production of fuels to total UK fuel consumption (defined as energy uses, non-energy uses and marine bunkers). As our ratio includes non-energy uses of fuels it is, strictly speaking, a fuel rather than an energy self-sufficiency

1

ratio and it includes marine bunkers as well as inland consumption. However, in the rest of this book we use the terms energy self-sufficiency and fuel self-sufficiency interchangeably to mean the ratio as just defined. Calculations of more restricted definitions of self-sufficiency (for example, production related only to inland energy consumption) can readily be derived from the two tables. We reserve comments on the economic significance of energy self-sufficiency for later chapters: the ratio is used in this chapter merely as a convenient summary statistic which illustrates fuel production and consumption movements over time.

In Tables 1.3 and 1.4 oil production and consumption statistics are given, and consumption is divided into main product groups. As with the previous tables, one cannot be sure that the statistics are precisely comparable throughout the period shown, but they are probably quite adequate as indicators of trends in the oil market. They are expressed in tonnes of oil[1], not tonnes of coal equivalent as in Tables 1.1 and 1.2. In Table 1.4, a self-sufficiency ratio is shown which is comparable to the ratios in Tables 1.1 and 1.2 in that it includes energy uses of oil, non-energy uses and marine bunkers.

Prewar trends in energy production and consumption

Britain's Industrial Revolution in the eighteenth and nineteenth centuries was fuelled by coal, and for many years thereafter the coal industry was the country's dominant producer of fuel. Not only did coal supply the needs of home consumers, but a very large export trade was built up in the latter part of the nineteenth century and the early years of this century. On the eve of the First World War in 1913, when the British coal industry was at the peak of its fortunes, it produced 292 million tonnes of coal, of which about one third (96 million tonnes) was either exported or supplied as bunkers to ships engaged in foreign trade. Subsequently, coal output was on a generally declining trend, as Figure 1 illustrates and as later parts of this chapter explain.

During the 1914-1918 War annual coal output fell to about 230 million tonnes. After a recovery in the early 1920s, production then tended to decline during the rest of the interwar

2

period. As Table 1.1 shows, between 1923 (the post First World War output peak) and 1938 coal production dropped from 280 to about 230 million tonnes, even though home consumption of coal remained almost unchanged at approximately 180 million tonnes. It was the previously large export trade which suffered in these years: coal sales for export and for marine bunkers halved from nearly 100 million tonnes in 1923 to about 50 million tonnes in 1938.

In the 1920s and 1930s oil accounted for almost the whole of the small increase in United Kingdom energy consumption from 188 to 196 mtce (Table 1.1), although there was an increase in production of hydro electricity from its negligible level in the early 1920s. Oil consumption, which was less than 4 million tonnes in 1923 (about 6 mtce, as indicated in Table 1.1), increased by 1938 to over 9 million tonnes (16 mtce) including non-energy uses. However, substitution of oil for coal had hardly begun in prewar Britain where in 1938 coal consumption was still about 92 per cent of total energy consumption (Table 1.1). Oil was in those days primarily a transport fuel. Motor spirit sales of nearly 5 million tonnes were well over 50 per cent of home oil consumption (Table 1.3), and non-energy uses of oil (mainly lubricating oil and bitumen) were another 15 per cent of the total. Fuel oil consumption (including refinery fuel and losses) was then only some 900,000 tonnes. Indigenous oil output, which was almost entirely from shale, was very small in relation to consumption and falling; from its 1923 peak of 228 thousand tonnes it had by 1938 declined to 128 thousand tonnes (Table 1.3). During the interwar years the United Kingdom's position as a major net exporter of energy was significantly eroded (Table 1.1). In 1923 home production of fuel of 280 million tonnes was about one third in excess of home consumption and marine bunkers, giving a fuel self-sufficiency ratio of 1.35; by 1938 production had fallen to around 230 million tonnes and the self-sufficiency ratio was down to 1.1.

The Second World War years and the early postwar period

There was a further decline in the British coal industry during the Second World War, when output

3

(including by then opencast as well as deep-mined coal) dropped to as low as 187 million tonnes in 1945, followed by a short-lived revival up to the mid-1950s. Production of deep-mined and opencast coal reached its postwar maximum of about 230 million tonnes in 1952.

In the early postwar years, although energy consumption was higher than in the years just before the war, the pattern of consumption had apparently changed little (Table 1.1). Coal accounted for almost 90 per cent of the 228 mtce of energy consumed in 1950 and oil almost all the remaining 10 per cent. However, the United Kingdom was no longer a net exporter of fuel. Declining home production of coal at a time of increasing fuel consumption meant that the self-sufficiency ratio fell from 1.1 in 1930 to 0.92 in 1950 (Table 1.1). Another significant change which is revealed by Table 1.3 is the considerable alteration in the composition of oil consumption - especially the growth of fuel oil consumption to over four times its 1938 level. In 1950 fuel oil sales were over 25 per cent of home oil sales compared with less than 10 per cent of the total in 1938; at the same time the share of motor spirit in the total fell (partly because of rationing) from 53 to 34 per cent.

The growth of oil, 1950 to 1973

Much more fundamental changes occurred in the energy market between 1950 and 1973. During those years real GNP was growing at an average compound rate of some 2½ per cent per annum and UK energy consumption (measured in coal equivalent) was increasing at nearly 2 per cent per annum. Nevertheless, within this expanding market the British coal industry experienced absolute decline at an unprecedented rate. Coal production fell from 219 million tonnes in 1950 to only 132 million tonnes in 1973 (Table 1.2), as home consumption dropped sharply and net exports fell to virtually zero. Coal's share in total energy consumption which had been 90 per cent in 1950 was just below 38 per cent in 1973.

The position of dominance which coal had maintained in industrial Britain for two hundred years from the mid-eighteenth century onwards was undermined in the post Second World War period principally by relatively low-priced oil. World

4

crude oil prices fell in real terms in the 1950s and even more so in the 1960s[2], at a time when costs and prices in the British coal industry were increasing. Transportation, refining, distribution and marketing unit costs also declined in the oil industry as the volumes sold increased enormously. As the price of oil fell relative to the price of coal, the range of uses of oil widened and further changes in production, transportation and consumption technology were stimulated. In Britain, as in other industrial countries, the rate of growth of oil sales was remarkable - nearly 9 per cent per annum compound between 1950 and 1973. Fuel oil, which was the fastest growing major product and the one which made inroads into industrial coal sales, grew even faster, at over 11 per cent per annum. By 1973 fuel oil sales were about 44 per cent of total home consumption of oil (Table 1.4).

British coal suffered also from the transformation of the gas industry brought about first by the move from coal to oil gasification and then by the discoveries of natural gas in the southern North Sea in the mid-1960s[3] which reduced prices and allowed gas to penetrate new markets. By 1973 natural gas had 12 per cent of the UK energy market (Table 1.2). There was also some expansion of nuclear power in the 1960s[4], though the share of nuclear electricity in energy consumption was only about 3 per cent in 1973. Despite the expansion of natural gas and nuclear power, indigenous fuel output fell a little from 1960 to 1973 and the self-sufficiency ratio dropped from 0.7 to about 0.5 (Table 1.2) as dependence on imported oil increased.

Increasing self-sufficiency 1973-83[5]

The discoveries of oil in the North Sea from about 1969 onwards led to a reversal of the trends of the late 1950s and 1960s. Instead of falling home production at a time of rising home consumption, production rose sharply at a time of falling consumption.

Table 1.2 illustrates the considerable fall in UK fuel consumption from 382 mtce in 1973 to 328 mtce in 1983 (14 per cent) despite the rise of about 8 per cent in real GDP during the period. Oil consumption dropped even more substantially, by some 36 per cent. Coal sales declined by about

17 per cent, but consumption of natural gas and nuclear electricity continued to rise. The fall in oil sales was unevenly distributed across the range of oil products (Table 1.4), partly because of widely varying rates of price increase and differing price elasticities of demand. Sales of fuel oil, which had risen so rapidly in the 1960s, dropped sharply by almost two thirds between 1973 and 1983. Sales of non-energy products - especially naphtha for petrochemical plants - also dropped substantially, as did consumption of naphtha at gasworks (included in 'other' in Table 1.4). Motor spirit sales, however, after declining a little between 1973 and 1976, resumed their rise: their share of home oil consumption increased from less than 16 per cent in 1973 to about 28 per cent in 1983. There was indeed a general and predictable tendency for consumption of oil products used for transport purposes to be less affected by the events of the 1970s than products more closely in competition with other fuels: sales of aviation turbine fuel and derv fuel, for instance, both increased a little between 1973 and 1983.

North Sea production started in 1975 and increased at remarkable speed until by 1983 it was much greater, in coal equivalent terms, than coal output (Table 1.2). In 1983 oil production (including very small but increasing onshore output) was nearly 115 million tonnes which, as Table 1.4 indicates, was about 42 million tonnes in excess of home consumption and marine bunkers. British North Sea gas output also increased in this period (Table 1.2), although it was insufficient to meet home demand and considerable volumes of gas were imported from Norway. By 1983 the total production of oil and gas from the British North Sea was around 250 mtce or about 75 per cent of total fuel consumption of 328 mtce. Coal production continued to fall gradually from 1973 onwards, although there was some increase in exports in the early 1980s. Output of nuclear electricity increased but it amounted to only 6 per cent of energy consumption in 1983.

As oil production increased rapidly in the late 1970s and early 1980s, the trend of the self-sufficiency ratio - which had fallen from 0.92 in 1950 to 0.49 in 1973 - was sharply reversed (Table 1.2). By 1983 it had risen to 1.19 and the United Kingdom was once more a significant net exporter of fuel, as it had been

before the 1939-45 War (Table 1.1). Then fuel
production had been almost entirely coal and
Britain was still a major coal exporter. In 1983,
however, the coal industry contributed only about
30 per cent of the country's fuel output (Table
1.2) and only about 7 million tonnes were
exported; most fuel exports were in the form of
oil. The self-sufficiency ratio for oil alone was
almost 1.6, whereas it had been virtually zero ten
years earlier (Table 1.4). Net exports of oil in
1983 of 42 million tonnes were equivalent to about
71 million tonnes of coal. Gross exports of crude
oil were far higher at around 67 million tonnes
(114 mtce), since the price premium attached to
North Sea crude because of its relatively high
quality made it advantageous to export about 60
per cent of output and bring in cheaper crudes to
meet the pattern of United Kingdom oil product
demand.

Notes

1. United Kingdom energy statistics for prewar and early postwar years are expressed in long tons but for the sake of comparability all the tables in this chapter are in (metric) tonnes. Where necessary, statistics originally expressed in tons have been converted to tonnes, using the factor:

1 long ton = 1.016 tonnes.

The conversion factors to coal equivalent are those used in the Department of Energy's annual Digest of UK Energy Statistics.

2. See Colin Robinson, 'The Changing Energy Market: What can we learn from the last ten years?' in D. Hawdon (ed.), The Energy 'Crisis': Ten Years After, Croom Helm, London, 1984.

3. Jonathan P. Stern, Gas's Contribution to UK Self-Sufficiency, BIJEPP Paper No. 10, Heinemann, London, 1984.

4. Richard Eden and Nigel Evans, Electricity's Contribution to UK Self-Sufficiency, BIJEPP Paper No. 11, Heinemann, London, 1984.

5. The early history of North Sea oil discoveries is discussed in Colin Robinson and Jon Morgan, North Sea Oil in the Future: Economic Analysis and Government Policy, Macmillan, London, 1978. The more recent history of oil production and consumption in the UK is analysed in Colin Robinson and Eileen Marshall, Oil's Contribution to UK Self-Sufficiency, BIJEPP Paper No. 12, Heinemann, London, 1984, chap. 1.

Table 1.1: UK fuel production and consumption 1923, 1938 and 1950

	1923 mtce	1923 % of total	1938 mtce	1938 % of total	1950 mtce	1950 % of total
FUEL PRODUCTION						
Coal	280	100	231	100	219	100
Oil	–	–	–	–	–	–
Hydro	–	–	1	–	1	–
TOTAL	280	100	232	100	220	100
FUEL CONSUMPTION						
Energy Uses:						
Coal	182	97	181	92	204	90
Oil	6	3	14	7	23	10
Hydro	–	–	1	1	1	–
TOTAL ENERGY USES	188	100	196	100	228	100
Non-energy uses of Oil	–		2		3	
Marine bunkers:						
Coal	18		11		4	
Oil	2		2		4	
TOTAL CONSUMPTION	208		211		239	
SELF-SUFFICIENCY RATIO	1.35		1.10		0.92	

Source: Department of Energy, Digest of UK Energy Statistics (various issues);
Ministry of Fuel and Power, Statistical Digest 1948-51.

Notes: – means nil, less than ½ million tonnes or less than ½ per cent;
mtce means million tonnes coal equivalent.
the self-sufficiency ratio is total production divided by total
consumption.

Table 1.2: UK fuel production and consumption, 1950 - 1983

	1950 mtce	1950 % of total	1960 mtce	1960 % of total	1973 mtce	1973 % of total	1983 mtce	1983 % of total
FUEL PRODUCTION								
Coal	219	100	198	99	132	70	119	30
Oil	-	-	-	-	1	1	195	50
Hydro	1	-	2	1	2	1	2	1
Nuclear	-	-	1	1	10	5	18	5
Natural Gas	-	-	-	-	43	23	56	14
TOTAL	220	100	201	100	188	100	390	100
FUEL CONSUMPTION								
Energy uses:								
Coal	204	90	199	74	133	38	111	35
Oil	23	10	68	25	164	46	106	34
Hydro	1	-	2	1	2	1	2	1
Nuclear	-	-	1	-	10	3	18	6
Natural Gas	-	-	-	-	44	12	74	24
TOTAL ENERGY USES	228	100	270	100	353	100	311	100
Non-energy uses of oil	3		7		20		14	
Marine bunkers:								
Coal	4		-		-		-	
Oil	4		9		9		3	
TOTAL CONSUMPTION	239		286		382		328	
SELF-SUFFICIENCY RATIO	0.92		0.70		0.49		1.19	

Source: Department of Energy, Digest of UK Energy Statistics (various issues) and Energy Trends (various issues).

Notes: see Table 1.1.

Table 1.3: UK oil production and consumption 1923, 1938 and 1950

Thousand tonnes

	1923	1938	1950
OIL PRODUCTION[a]	228	128	160
HOME OIL CONSUMPTION			
Motor spirit	1,080[c]	4,908	5,278
Kerosene	540[c]	733	1,564
Gas/Diesel	(1,810[c]	1,203	2,671
Fuel oil[b]	(	900	3,961
Non-energy uses	(420[c]	1,346	1,670
Other	(	117	536
TOTAL	3,850[c]	9,207	15,680
MARINE BUNKERS	959	1,354	2,264
HOME CONSUMPTION AND BUNKERS	4,809[c]	10,561	17,944

a including shale oil
b including refinery fuel and losses (partly estimated for some years)
c partly estimated

Source: Ministry of Fuel and Power, Statistical Digests 1948-51

Table 1.4: UK oil production and consumption, 1950 - 1983

	1950	1960	Thousand tonnes 1973	1983[e]
OIL PRODUCTION	160[a]	148[a]	372[d]	11,4917[d]
HOME OIL CONSUMPTION				
Motor spirit	5,278	7,747	16,927	19,566
Kerosene	1,564	2,402	7,421	6,242
Gas/Diesel	2,671	6,220	20,758	16,662
Fuel oil[b]	3,961	22,017	47,832	18,526
Non-energy uses	1,670	4,090	11,149	7,810
Other	536	1,805	3,642	2,100
TOTAL	15,680	44,281	107,729	70,906
MARINE BUNKERS	2,264	5,514	5,499	1,881
HOME CONSUMPTION AND BUNKERS	17,944	49,795	113,228	72,787
SELF SUFFICIENCY RATIO[c]	-	-	-	1.58

Note: In some years total oil consumption as shown in this table is slightly different from its equivalent (in mtce) in Table 1.2 because of stock changes and minor statistical differences.

a   including shale oil
b   including refinery fuel and losses
c   oil production divided by home consumption and bunkers
d   including condensates, ethane, propane and butane
e   partly estimated

Source: Department of Energy, Digest of UK Energy Statistics (various issues) and Energy Trends (various issues).

12

FIGURE 1   UK COAL PRODUCTION
                       1900-1983
                   MILLION TONNES

Chapter Two

SELF-SUFFICIENCY AND FUEL POLICY

Was self-sufficiency an aim of policy?

One question which arises from the description of energy trends in Chapter 1 is whether governments deliberately promoted self-sufficiency as one of the objectives of fuel policy. During the interwar period, Britain was a net exporter of energy (Table 1.1), but in the twenty-five years after the Second World War the fuel self-sufficiency ratio fell to about 0.5, only to climb again to well over 1 by the early 1980s. Though the part which government policies played in these changes cannot be precisely quantified, one can examine policy statements in an attempt to uncover the underlying motivations and to assess the significance attached to various aims. Below we review the salient features of British government fuel policies in the postwar years[1] and draw some conclusions about the weight which was placed on fuel self-sufficiency as an objective.

Nationalisation and statements of fuel policy

From the earliest postwar years British governments had policies of one sort or another towards the energy industries. The Labour government elected in 1945 nationalised the three energy industries whose activities were principally within Britain. In 1947 the National Coal Board was given a statutory monopoly of coal production (except for some 'licensed mines'); also in 1947 the British Electricity Authority and the North of Scotland Hydro Electric Board obtained a monopoly of the supply of electricity for public sale in Britain; and in 1948 the Gas Council and Area Boards gained sole rights to the delivery of gas through pipes in Britain. Creation of these public fuel corporations was, however, one element in the early postwar drive to nationalise what were perceived to be key industries ('commanding heights') rather than part of a specific policy towards fuel.

Coherent statements of government fuel policy are indeed few and far between in the postwar period. It was not until October 1965 that the first postwar White Paper on Fuel Policy[2] was published by the Labour government of the time, though there had been some energy industry targets in the September 1965 National Plan[3]. The 1965 White Paper was quickly followed in 1967 by another White Paper[4] which was a much more systematic exposition of policy. A long gap followed until the Labour governments of the mid-1970s published a number of papers on fuel policy and fuel forecasts, notably a Green Paper in 1978[5]. Most recently, a paper prepared in 1982 by the Department of Energy[6] for the Sizewell PWR Inquiry contains a statement of the principles of energy policy as seen by the 1979-83 Conservative government. To describe British fuel policy in the postwar period these few explicit statements need to be supplemented by a great deal of study of ministerial pronouncements and of those government actions which had an impact on the nationalised and private corporations in the energy sector.

The early postwar years

In the early postwar years the dominant position of coal (Table 1.2) meant that fuel policy and coal policy were virtually synonymous. As a PEP study explains

> During those early postwar years the country's fuel problem was seen as achieving a recovery in British coal production sufficient to furnish the rapidly rising fuel requirements of general industrial recovery in the economy. Oil and other imports were thought of strictly in terms of making up 'the energy gap' between what the newly-nationalised coalmining industry could manage and the amounts that fuel consumers demanded.[7]

At that time there was still some hankering after self-sufficiency; for a few years after the War the belief still lingered that the British coal industry might achieve and even exceed the output and exports of the immediate prewar years.

As explained in Chapter 1, there was a brief period in the early 1950s when coal production did rise to approximately its 1930 level. However, it was already becoming clear that British coal would be unable to meet the anticipated increase in fuel consumption[8]. The Ridley Committee[9], reporting in 1952, forecast that UK coal consumption would increase up to the early 1960s but that oil would increase its share of the energy market. In the event, Ridley substantially over-estimated coal consumption and under-estimated oil consumption in the early 1960s; the Committee's forecast errors are hardly surprising considering that its report was written in the very early stages of the switch from coal to oil.

From the late 1950s to the late 1960s

By the late 1950s, British coal production was falling and even a small expansion of the industry no longer seemed feasible[10]. From that time onwards both Conservative and Labour governments implicitly accepted that the coal industry would contract. Governments were unwilling to commit themselves to a minimum coal production target, despite considerable pressure from the National Union of Mineworkers and the National Coal Board for a commitment to 200 million tonnes a year. Nevertheless, they did provide support for coal on an increasing scale in an attempt to moderate its rate of decline.

Politicians were at first unwilling to admit openly that coal, the country's only large indigenous fuel supplier, had resumed its long-term decline and that there was little they could do about it. The government machine thus acted, as it frequently does, with a series of instant responses to problems which in the late 1950s and early 1960s seemed urgent. No attempt seems to have been made to formulate a coherent strategy. Indeed, Ministers probably felt that publication of an explicit fuel policy - which would inevitably have contained forecasts of a declining coal industry - would have caused them serious political problems. It was not until the 1965 and 1967 Fuel Policy White Papers appeared (by which time the long-run nature of the decline in coal

was quite obvious) that any serious attempt was
made to justify the policy of protection for coal
and other indigenous fuels which had evolved in
the previous ten years.

The two White Papers can best be seen as ex
post justifications for a rather haphazard
collection of government measures affecting the
fuel industries which had accumulated since the
late 1950s[11], rather than as a new look at
policy. The principal instrument which affected
the terms of competition among the fuel industries
was a tax of 0.9p per gallon on fuel and heating
oils (equivalent to over 30 per cent of the then
pre-tax price of heavy fuel oil) which protected
coal from oil competition, and incidentally also
protected nuclear power and natural gas from oil.
The confusion which surrounded fuel 'policy' in
this period can readily be appreciated from the
remark made by the Chancellor (then Mr Selwyn
Lloyd) on introducing the fuel oil tax in his 1961
Budget, that it was purely a 'revenue duty'.

Several important steps affecting natural
gas and nuclear power had also been taken in the
1950s and early 1960s. For instance, the first
civil nuclear power programme, started in 1955,
was expanded to 5000 MW in 1957 after the 1956
Suez crisis, apparently in an effort to make
energy supplies more secure; by the mid-1960s
there was a second nuclear programme aiming at the
construction of 8000 MW of Advanced Gas Cooled
Reactor stations by 1975. The Continental Shelf
Act of 1964 strengthened the monopoly position of
the nationalised gas industry by making it de
facto sole buyer of any natural gas discovered in
the North Sea[12], and the 'discretionary' system of
North Sea licence allocation was also instituted
in 1964.

Other measures, which were primarily intended
to protect coal, were a ban on coal imports, a
virtual ban on Soviet oil imports, and preference
for coal both in the important electricity
generation market and in the local authority
market. Assistance for the coal industry and its
employees was also provided, by a £415 million
debt write-off for the National Coal Board in a
capital reconstruction in 1965 and government aid
for miners displaced by the contraction of the
industry. The 'policy' which emerged, however,
did more than protect the coal industry.[13] North
Sea gas and nuclear power both gained from the
taxation of one of their principal competitors

17

Fuel policy

(fuel oil), and even the oil companies were to some extent sheltered from competition because of the exclusion of Soviet oil and US coal. Thus the whole British fuel market was protected from overseas competition, though the degree of protection was undoubtedly greatest for coal.

The reasons given in the 1965 and 1967 White Papers to justify the policy of favouring indigenous fuel industries were as follows. According to the White Papers, indigenous fuels have less impact on the balance of payments, they are more secure than imported energy, they provide some insurance against the possibility of a future oil shortage, and coal protection is specifically justified because of the considerable social and human costs of a contracting coal industry.

Whether or not one accepts that these stated reasons constitute the real origins of the policy of protectionism is not a matter we think it relevant to pursue in this paper[14]. The principal point we wish to establish is that, from the late 1950s to the late 1960s, though governments for a variety of reasons protected indigenous fuel industries, circumstances were such that no government could contemplate a policy of self-sufficiency (in the sense of aiming at a self-sufficiency ratio of around 1). Immediately after the Second World War when coal still had over 90 per cent of the energy market (Table 1.2) such a policy might have seemed achievable at low economic and political cost. But, in the period we are considering, governments baulked at the swingeing measures which would have been necessary in pursuit of a self-sufficiency policy - for instance, much higher taxes on oil, more subsidisation of coal, more promotion of nuclear power, even stricter controls on public sector fuel purchasers to make sure they burned coal, and even perhaps some form of fuel rationing. The opportunity costs of moving resources into coal and nuclear electricity production and away from other sectors of the economy must have seemed too great[15]; the political disadvantages of restricting consumers' freedom of fuel choice and raising their costs must have appeared quite out of proportion to any benefits which might accrue.

Governments therefore settled for a 'satisficing' compromise which they hoped would just satisfy the mining industry and the industries associated with nuclear power without antagonising fuel consumers too much. In the process, Britain became less self-sufficient in fuel during the 1960s (though the self-sufficiency ratio was almost certainly somewhat higher than if governments had eschewed intervention in the fuel market, mainly because some high-cost coal mines were kept in operation). But the period was one in which self-sufficiency seemed so far out of reach and its pursuit appeared so costly that it was no longer the live issue it had been in the early postwar years.

Policy from the late 1960s onwards

For five or six years after publication of the 1967 White Paper there were no significant changes in British fuel policy although the trend towards increasing support for indigenously-produced fuels continued. The fuel oil tax was raised (though not in real terms) to about 1p per gallon in 1968, the NCB's accumulated deficits were written off after the miners' strikes of 1972 and 1973-74, the value of its assets was written down again in 1973, and the 1973 Coal Industry Act provided for £720 million in grants to the Board during the subsequent five years.

The UK's fuel situation was, however, beginning to change considerably as it moved towards what the 1967 White Paper described as a 'four-fuel economy'. The second nuclear power programme of 8000 MW was under way and at that time completion was expected by the mid-1970s. More important, North Sea natural gas production began in 1968 and increased rapidly during the government's policy of rapid exploitation under which there was little official interference with the oil companies' gas depletion programmes. Governments of the time wanted to ease the perceived balance of payments constraint on the British economy and evidently believed that the economic benefit of the gas discoveries would be maximised by

> ... exploiting and extracting ... as quickly as possible.[16]

Growing supplies of natural gas and nuclear electricity were expected to limit the growth of oil, and the Labour governments of the late 1960s seemed quite prepared to accept a relatively small further reduction in the fuel self-sufficiency ratio. In the words of the 1967 White Paper (paragraph 88),

With a four-fuel economy the proportion of its energy requirements for which the country has to rely on imported fuel in the mid-1970s would be little higher than it is today, and there should be no greater need to consider limiting the growth of oil on security grounds.

Even more radical changes in the United Kingdom's energy position occurred, however, as the first discoveries of oil were made in the North Sea from 1969 onwards. Substantial recoverable reserves of oil were discovered in the 1969-76 period and it was becoming clear that within a few years Britain might cease to be a net importer of crude oil. At the end of 1972 a memorandum to the Commons Public Accounts Committee[17] suggested oil production from the United Kingdom's sector of the North Sea might be 75 million tonnes in 1980, and by May 1975 the annual Brown Book[18] had raised that estimate to 100-130 million tonnes. Since the government estimated oil consumption in the early 1980s at about 120 million tonnes[19], self-sufficiency appeared to be in prospect by that time, although there were few people who anticipated the size of the oil export surplus which actually appeared (Table 1.4) as oil consumption dropped sharply from 1973 onwards, falling to only 72 million tonnes in 1983.

Coincidentally, as the United Kingdom discovered much larger offshore resources of hydrocarbons than had been anticipated in the 1960s, the oil price 'shocks' of the 1970s occurred and led to general concern about the possibility of future oil shortages and to unease about dependence on imported oil. Thus, just as the internal energy situation was changing, the energy environment within which the United Kingdom operates altered fundamentally. Energy policy had seemed to be an issue for specialists only during the 1960s, when the ready availability of low-priced oil and the absence of serious supply interruptions pushed into the background any concern about fuel supplies. Public awareness of energy matters was, however, greatly increased from 1973 onwards as the news media turned their attention to the oil market, treating the oil-producing countries of OPEC and oil consumers in the industrialised world as adversaries. Shortages of petrol, electricity and other fuels all focussed public attention on the energy market.

Consequently, the 'energy issue' crossed the threshold of public awareness and politicians in Britain and abroad felt it necessary to produce policies which would convince the electorate that they were active in dealing with the problems which had emerged. The International Energy Agency (consisting of the OECD nations other than Finland, France and Iceland) was established in 1974, and the energy 'crisis' assumed such importance that world leaders met to discuss the problems of world energy (as at the Tokyo summit in June 1979).

In Britain, where North Sea discoveries and miners' strikes as well as the actions of OPEC received widespread media attention, there was considerable government activity in the mid-1970s, much of it concerned with offshore oil. The British National Oil Corporation, established by the 1975 Petroleum and Submarine Pipelines Act, was intended to bring a State presence into the oil industry. It had certain privileges as compared with the private sector oil companies (such as exemption from Petroleum Revenue Tax and representation on oilfield operating committees) and there were some overtones of self-sufficiency in its activities; for instance, 51 per cent State 'participation' gave BNOC the right to purchase over half the oil produced in the North Sea[20]. A new development in policy was the convening in June 1976 of a National Energy Conference by the then Secretary of State for Energy (Mr Benn). In 1977 an Energy Commission was instituted and received large numbers of policy documents, and in 1978 a Green Paper on Energy Policy appeared.

Policy towards the British coal industry also changed after the 1973 oil price increases, although the changes were modifications of existing measures rather than new departures. The government endorsed the National Coal Board's 1974 Plan for Coal and its 1977 successor Coal for the Future which aimed at expanding the industry; according to Coal for the Future, output in the year 2000 would increase to 170 million tonnes[21]. Subsidisation of coal continued and the fuel oil tax was raised from 1p per gallon to 2.5p in 1977, 3p in 1979 and 3.5p in 1980. The Conservative administration of 1979-83 at first seemed to aim at a progressive reduction in support for British coal, passing the Coal Industry Act of 1980 which would have eliminated NCB deficit grants by 1983-84. However, after a threatened national

strike in February 1981 support for the coal
industry was increased and coal imports were
severely limited[22]. Given the uncertain world
energy environment, it is hardly surprising that
in the 1970s and early 1980s a major indigenous
fuel producer such as the British coal industry
should have perceived itself as having sufficient
bargaining power to oppose government policy.
However, that power began to fade in 1982 and 1983
as the prices of internationally-traded fossil
fuels weakened, Britain became self-sufficient in
oil, and there was once again considerable over-
production of British coal. By late 1983 and
early 1984 the Coal Board (under Mr MacGregor, its
new Chairman) and the government were prepared to
sit out a long overtime ban and a period of
strikes by the National Union of Mineworkers
against proposed pit closures (see Chapter 5).

It was not only the British coal industry
which, for a time at least, gained from a revival
of interest in indigenous fuel resources because
of the perceived uncertainty of imported oil
supplies. The European Economic Community set
targets for oil import reductions by its members
and urged that indigenous fuel supplies
(especially coal and nuclear) should be increased
wherever possible, as well as stressing the need
for vigorous pursuit of 'conservation'. The
International Energy Agency produced similar
messages: its annual review of member countries'
'policies and programmes'[23] invariably contains
exhortations to stimulate domestic fuel supplies,
to conserve energy and to minimise oil imports.

This apparent international consensus about
the virtues of greater reliance on indigenous
energy resources (and, by implication, the virtues
of increasing self-sufficiency ratios) was echoed
in British policy documents of the period. Britain
by the late 1970s was in a unique position among
large Western industrial countries by being on the
verge of self-sufficiency. Thus the tone of
policy statements was very different from that of
the 1967 Fuel Policy White Paper which, as we have
seen, was content to accept gradually rising
import dependence. Britain evidently had some
discretion over its degree of self-sufficiency and
over the period during which it would remain self-
sufficient. This view that Britain now had more
degrees of freedom in fuel policy was expressed,
for example, in a 1978 Department of Energy paper
on offshore oil policy[24] which stated that

The Government's initial priority has been the attainment, as early as practicable, of net self-sufficiency in energy. We expect to become self-sufficient in 1980. Thereafter there is likely to be some choice between early oil production at higher levels, with associated early additional benefits for the economy, and reserving supplies for the 1990s and beyond to assist the economy, and the energy sector, in achieving a smooth transition to reliance on renewed import of oil likely then to be scarcer and more expensive, or alternative indigenous fuels.

In 1977 the Department had expressed a similar view in its Energy Policy Review[25].

The re-awakening of interest in self-sufficiency in the industrialised world in the 1970s and early 1980s is clearly a product of the environment of those years. In Britain, the desire to raise the self-sufficiency ratio, which was common to most countries, was reinforced by the ability to do so. British governments created an environment in which the oil companies could proceed with development of the substantial reserves they had located in the early 1970s, and by the efforts of the companies self-sufficiency was achieved at remarkable speed. First production from the North Sea was in late 1975, in which year the fuel self-sufficiency ratio (as defined in Chapter 1) was 0.57; by 1981 the ratio had risen to 1.05 and by 1983 to 1.19.

Fuel self-sufficiency, once in sight and then attained, evidently generated some desire for its own perpetuation. In popular discussion, there was appeal in the idea that dependence on foreigners for such a vital commodity as fuel might be avoided for a long period. Moreover, politicians, who often seek apparently simple, quantifiable and achievable targets, found the idea of prolonging self-sufficiency attractive. The reasons which had previously been given in Britain to justify protection of indigenous fuel industries, and especially coal (see above), appeared again in the policy documents of the late 1970s in support of a policy of maintaining self-sufficiency. Furthermore, there are hints in these documents of a desire for self-sufficiency per se[26]. Some sections of the 1978 Energy Policy Green Paper suggest that fuel import minimisation was then seen as an important objective in its own

right.   In an Annex to that Paper[27], in Energy
Projections 1979[28] and in a document presented to
the Vale of Belvoir Public Inquiry in 1979[29], the
Department of Energy produced calculations of the
extent to which indigenous fuel supplies would be
capable of meeting end-century UK primary fuel
demand.   The implication seemed to be that imports
should be regarded as a second-best alternative to
indigenous supplies.[30]

The Conservative administration from mid-1979
onwards   clearly   believed   that   the   import
'gapology' of Labour's policy documents had been
misguided.   The Energy Department's Sizewell
evidence[31] takes a very different line from the
Department's   statements   in   the   late   1970s,
stressing the importance of increasing competition
in the energy market and allowing market forces to
regulate supply and demand.   There is a specific
disclaimer of any intention to pursue fuel self-
-sufficiency per se (paragraph 5 of the Annex);

> Not only is it unwise to take a single view
> of the future, it is also unnecessary to
> envisage   supplying   the   country's   needs
> totally   from   domestic   production.   This
> country has a long history as a trading
> nation.   It may prove economic to import some
> fuels which are expensive to produce at home
> and to plan for profitable exports where
> suitable opportunities arise.   Furthermore,
> future mis-matches of demand and supply for
> tradeable energy products may be accommodated
> by imports and exports at world prices.

The Conservatives' views on self-sufficiency
are at variance not only with those of the 1974-79
Labour government but apparently also with those
of the International Energy Agency which, as we
have mentioned, constantly exhorts its members to
minimise oil imports.   In the Agency's 1982 Review
of British policy, its rapporteur obviously finds
difficulty   in   understanding   why   the   British
government is unwilling to publish 'most probable'
supply and demand forecasts and why it has not
formulated '... a broad policy framework including
a longer term supply picture'.[32]

The   Conservatives,   however,   were   more
inclined   to   inject   competition   into   the   fuel
market than to publish forecasts and plans.   From
1982 onwards a number of steps were taken which
could have significant long-run effects on the
fuel market and therefore on self-sufficiency.

The British Gas Corporation's monopoly and monopsony powers[33] were reduced under the terms of the Oil and Gas (Enterprise) Act of 1982 and the government decided to sell off BGC's oil production assets; the British National Oil Corporation's State trading arm was separated from its exploration and production activities, the latter becoming Britoil with 51 per cent of its shares in private hands and no special privileges as compared with other oil companies; the government announced that it would not for the time being implement any depletion control measures[34]; there were minor measures to facilitate the private generation and distribution of electricity in the 1982 Energy Act; and even the coal industry's protection seemed threatened after publication of a critical Monopolies Commission report[35] and the appointment of a new Chairman of the NCB. A number of newspaper reports[36] suggested that parts of both the electricity and gas industries were candidates for 'privatisation' in the mid-1980s.

Conclusions

We would conclude that interest in fuel self-sufficiency in the United Kingdom has waxed and waned during the postwar period as perceptions of the attainability of self-sufficiency and of the security of overseas fuel supplies have changed; more recently, it has also varied according to the political party in office. In the early postwar years when home-produced coal supplied the bulk of Britain's fuel, it seemed for a brief period that home fuel supplies could keep pace with demand. That belief faded with the advent of low-cost oil, and interest in self-sufficiency as a policy target faded too: politicians have no incentive to set targets which are clearly unattainable at reasonable cost. Governments in the 1960s therefore concentrated on policies of tempering the effects of fuel market forces, primarily to avoid too rapid a decline in the coal industry; in the process they also protected other fuel industries and the self-sufficiency ratio was slightly raised compared with what it would have been in a more competitive market.

Two events in the 1970s revived interest in a self-sufficiency policy. First, the two oil

25

'shocks' gave rise to a very uncertain world energy environment in which oil imports in particular became much more expensive and apparently less secure from interruption; thus there seemed to be advantage in reducing oil import dependence. Second, the discovery of considerable oil reserves in the British sector of the North Sea brought fuel self-sufficiency within reach. In these circumstances, the question of achieving and prolonging self-sufficiency inevitably became a policy issue and it revealed differences in philosophy between the Labour and Conservative parties.

The present government has adopted a generally non-interventionist stance in the energy market and seems ready to accept whatever degree of self-sufficiency results from the more competitive market at which it is aiming. However, as Britain's fuel export surplus begins to decline, as it probably will from the mid-1980s onwards, and as the country moves towards becoming a net importer once more, a debate is likely on the rights and wrongs of intervention to prolong self-sufficiency. The purpose of the rest of this paper is, first, to set out what might happen to self-sufficiency up to our time horizon of 2020 in the absence of any government policy change, and second, to contribute to the debate on the advantages and disadvantages of using self-sufficiency as a policy target.

Notes

1.   For more detailed accounts see PEP, London, A Fuel Policy for Britain, Political and Economic Planning, 1966; M.V. Posner, Fuel Policy: A Study in Applied Economics, Macmillan, London, 1973; and Colin Robinson, A Policy for Fuel? Institute of Economic Affairs, London, 1969, Competition for Fuel, Institute of Economic Affairs, 1971, and The Energy 'Crisis' and British Coal, Institute of Economic Affairs, 1974.

2.   Fuel Policy, Cmnd. 2798, HMSO, London, October 1965.

3.   The National Plan, Cmnd. 2764, HMSO, London, September 1965.

4.   Fuel Policy, Cmnd. 3438, HMSO, London, November 1967.

5.   Energy Policy: A Consultative Document, Cmnd. 7101, HMSO, London, 1978.   Among other official papers of the same period were Energy Policy Review, Energy Paper no. 22, Department of Energy, 1977; Offshore Oil Policy, Energy Commission Paper no. 19, Department of Energy, 1978; and Energy Projections 1979, Department of Energy, 1979.

6.   Department of Energy, Proof of Evidence for the Sizewell 'B' Public Inquiry, October 1982.

7.   PEP, A Fuel Policy for Britain, op.cit, p. 14.

8.   Ibid. p. 15.

9.   Report of the Committee on National Policy for the Use of Fuel and Power Resources, Cmnd. 8647, HMSO, London, 1952.

10.   The National Coal Board itself revised downwards its coal output targets during the 1950s.   In 1950 it aimed to produce 240 million tonnes a year by 1961-65, but by 1959 its aim was production of 200-215 million tonnes a year in the 1960s. See PEP, op.cit., p. 117.

11.   Further discussion of the haphazard nature of policy in the late 1950s and 1960s is in Robinson, A Policy for Fuel?, op.cit., especially pp. 15-25.   The policy in force in 1969 is also explained there.

12.   Ibid. pp. 16-24.

13.   Ibid. p. 18.

14.   Ibid. argues that nationalism and a desire for government intervention were important unstated reasons for the policy of protection.

15.   In the words of the 1967 White Paper, 'excessive protection for coal would lead to a misallocation of manpower and capital to the detriment of the economy as a whole'. Cmnd. 3438, paragraph 89.   See also Robinson, The Energy 'Crisis' and British Coal, op.cit., pp. 42-47.

16.   See North Sea Oil and Gas, First Report from the Committee of Public Accounts, House of Commons, Session 1972-73, HMSO, London, paragraph 96, and Robinson and Morgan, op.cit., chap. 2.

17.   North Sea Oil and Gas, op.cit., Minutes of Evidence, 13 December 1972, Memorandum by the Department of Trade and Industry, p. 52.

18.   Development of the Oil and Gas Resources of the United Kingdom, Department of Energy, HMSO, London, 1975.

19.   House of Commons, Hansard, 6 December 1974, Written Answers, col. 647.

20.   The establishment of BNOC and its functions are discussed in Colin Robinson and Chris Rowland, 'North Sea Oil and Gas', in The Structure of British Industry, P.S. Johnson (ed.), Granada, London, 1980.

21.   A critique of the Coal Board's plans is in Robinson and Marshall, What Future for British Coal?   Institute of Economic Affairs, London, 1981.

22.   Ibid., chap. 1 and Prologue for details of the 1980 Act and the subsequent policy change.

23.   The latest edition is International Energy Agency, Energy Policies and Programmes of IEA Countries, 1982 Review, Paris, 1983.

24.   Offshore Oil Policy, op.cit., p. 6.

25.   Energy Policy Review, op.cit., paragraph 49 (ii).

26.   Such a desire would be consistent with the element of nationalism in British fuel policy which seemed evident in the earlier postwar period.   See Robinson, A Policy for Fuel?, op.cit., pp. 23-4.

27.   Cmnd. 7101, Annex 1.

28.   Energy Projections 1979, op.cit., paragraphs 25-9.

29.   Assessment of Energy Requirements, Department of Energy, Evidence to Vale of Belvoir Public Inquiry, July 1979.

30.   Robinson and Marshall, What Future for British Coal? op.cit., pp. 79-82 criticises these calculations.

31. Proof of Evidence for the Sizewell 'B' Public Inquiry, op.cit., especially pp. 1-5 and A1-A2.

32. Energy Policies and Programmes of IEA Countries: 1982 Review, op.cit., pp. 361-379.

33. The situation before the Act is described in Colin Robinson, 'The Errors of North Sea Policy', Lloyds Bank Review, July 1981.

34. See Robinson, 'Oil Depletion Policy in the United Kingdom', Three Banks Review, September 1982.

35. Monopolies and Mergers Commission, National Coal Board, Cmnd. 8920 (2 volumes) HMSO, London, June 1983.

36. For instance, 'Power supply review likely before sell-off', The Financial Times, 28 November 1983.

Chapter Three

ENERGY SELF-SUFFICIENCY TRENDS WITH UNCHANGED GOVERNMENT POLICY

The 'unchanged policy' assumption

We begin by defining 'unchanged policy', which we
take to be that set of government measures in
existence in early 1984 ('now') specifically
affecting the energy industries; where the
Conservative government had by early 1984 clearly
embarked on a course of action (such as the sale
of BGC oil assets) we have included it in policy
'now', even though it had not been completed. As
explained in Chapter 2, it is not easy to identify
exactly which measures constitute fuel policy, but
we have listed below those which seem most
important[1]. Our assumptions are as follows:

> Taxes: all taxes on fuel, whether on
> production or consumption, remain constant in
> real terms. For example, the petrol, derv
> and fuel oil duties (respectively 74.1, 62.8
> and 3.5 pence per gallon) rise in line with
> inflation, and VAT is at 15 per cent. The
> structure of taxation on oil production and
> the rates of tax remain as in the March 1983
> Budget[2], including the distinction between
> 'old' and 'new' oil fields.
> North Sea oil: there are no production cuts
> nor development delays imposed by government,
> Britoil and BNOC remain as at present
> constituted, the British Gas Corporation's
> onshore and offshore oil production assets
> are sold, as are its potentially oil-bearing
> offshore blocks. There is no other
> privatisation (or nationalisation). The
> discretionary licensing system remains the
> primary method of allocating rights to

explore for and produce oil, though there are occasional auctions and additional payments for self-selected blocks.

Gas: companies which discover gas in the UK offshore area can make direct sales to larger consumers as defined in the Oil and Gas (Enterprise) Act, but exports of gas are not permitted. There is no further reduction in BGC's monopoly/monopsony power and the Corporation is not privatised.

Coal: coal imports continue to be restricted to about 3-4 million tonnes a year. Deficit grants, other subsidies to the NCB and grants to mineworkers remain constant in real terms. The coal conversion scheme, due to end in December 1984, remains in being, with grants similar in real terms to those given under the original scheme. The Coal Board is not privatised.

Electricity: construction of the Sizewell 'B' Pressurised Water Reactor (PWR) begins in 1986 and thereafter the government acquiesces in a modest Central Electricity Generating Board programme of PWR building. Alternatively, more Advanced Gas Cooled Reactors (AGRs) are built instead of the PWRs. The nationalised electricity supply industry retains the main responsibility for electricity generation and distribution and is not privatised. The Atomic Energy Authority remains as at present constituted.

Renewables: government support for R and D into renewable energy forms continues at the same level in real terms as in recent years (about £12 million a year).

Demand side policies: governments continue to rely principally on fuel prices to give conservation incentives to consumers, though the present range of minor conservation subsidies remains in being.

In general, our 'unchanged policy' assumption implies a fairly market-oriented stance, but with no further privatisation of the nationalised fuel industries and with support for coal at its present level in real terms. On this assumption, we now consider trends in total fuel consumption, fuel production and the consequent self-sufficiency ratios up to our time horizon of 2020. Since the objective of this paper is primarily to analyse the principle of self-sufficiency as a policy aim, we discuss only the general direction and order of magnitude of likely production and consumption movements so as to provide the essential background for the analysis of later chapters. Other papers in this series examine in more detail the prospects for individual fuels.

Total energy and electricity consumption

For consistency with our fuel policy assumptions, in considering future energy consumption we assume that macro-economic policy continues along the same lines as practised by the Conservatives since 1979, giving priority to the minimisation of inflation. The resulting rate of increase of real GDP from 1982 to 2020 is assumed to be in the range 1 to 2 per cent per annum.

If we assume also that there are carry-over effects from past fuel price increases which will continue to induce consumers to conserve fuel in the 1980s and that there will be further small increases in real fuel prices, energy consumption is not likely to increase a great deal. After some recovery from its recession-affected level in 1982-83, primary fuel consumption in the United Kingdom might well rise at no more than ½ to 1 per cent per annum on average into the early part of next century. Primary fuel consumption would then be in the following ranges:

	mtce
1983	328
1990	345 - 360
2000	365 - 400
2010	385 - 440
2020	405 - 485

For comparison, the mid-point of the range for 2000 is about the same as the highest annual primary fuel consumption so far reached in the United Kingdom (382 mtce in 1973), and close to the 387 mtce estimate in the Department of Energy's Case BL in its Sizewell evidence[3] which assumes a real GDP growth rate in the middle of our 1-2 per cent per annum range.

Electricity consumption in the United Kingdom, which is an important determinant of coal and nuclear power output, is assumed in this chapter to increase at between ½ and 1½ per cent per annum in the period up to 2020. The Energy

Department's Case BL uses an electricity growth rate of about 1 per cent per annum from 1980 to 2010.

Coal production

After a period of relative stability from 1972 to 1980, British coal output was once more in decline from 1980 to 1983, with output falling from 130 to 119 million tonnes (Table 1.2). Inland consumption was, however, falling faster (111 million tonnes in 1983) and, despite some increase in exports, stocks were therefore mounting up to the time of the miners' industrial action which began in the autumn of 1983. In the next few years it seems likely that production will be reduced so that it is more closely in line with demand. On our unchanged government policy assumption, we would expect output to be on a declining trend during the rest of this century and into the early years of next century.

An assessment we made in 1981 of British coal prospects market-by-market[4] suggested that, with unchanged government policy, with electricity demand rising at $\frac{1}{2}$ to $1\frac{1}{2}$ per cent per annum, and with UK coal prices rising rather faster than oil prices up to the end of the century, UK coal consumption in the year 2000 would probably be in the range 75 to 110 million tonnes. UK production would be about the same since imports and exports were assumed to be small.

At that time both the Coal Board (170 million tonnes) and the Department of Energy (128-165 million tonnes) had very much higher coal forecasts for 2000. However, both organisations have greatly reduced their estimates. In 1982 the Coal Board gave an estimate of 113 to 142 million tonnes[5] and Mr Norman Siddall, when Chairman of the NCB, is reported to have said[6] that British coal production could be down to 100 million tonnes by 1990. The Energy Department's most recent published estimate[7] of coal consumption in the year 2000 is 100 to 140 million tonnes.

The NCB and Energy Department forecasts still seem to us to be on the high side, given our assumptions about government policy and the growth of electricity demand. For the purposes of this chapter we continue therefore to use our 75 to 110 million tonne production range both for 2000 and for 2010, with slightly lower figures for 2020.

33

Unchanged government policy

Our figures are as follows:

	million tonnes
1983	119
1990	95 - 115
2000	75 - 110
2010	75 - 110
2020	70 - 105

The British coal industry undoubtedly has the potential to exceed our estimates[8] but, on our unchanged policy assumption, we doubt whether that potential will be realised.

Oil production

Output of oil from the British sector of the North Sea has risen sharply from only about 1 million tonnes in 1975 to 115 million tonnes in 1983 (2.3 million barrels per day). Production was, however, by the early months of 1984 nearing its peak which will probably be somewhere in the range 2.5 to 2.6 million barrels per day. Annual output is likely to fluctuate in the range 110 to 120 million tonnes (2.2 to 2.4 million barrels a day) during the period 1984-86. Thereafter, a declining trend can be expected, though there may well be considerable variations because of the bunching of field developments and there are likely to be periods when production increases temporarily.

Future output depends not only on the geology of the North Sea but on trends in costs, prices and taxes. We have made oil production estimates in another volume in this series[9], assuming that the oil tax system remains as in the 1983 Budget and using two sets of price assumptions - one that real crude oil prices fall at about 1 per cent per annum up to our time horizon of 2020 and the other that real crude prices rise at $2\frac{1}{2}$ per cent per annum over the same period. The resulting oil production estimates which we use in this chapter (including small amounts of onshore oil production) are as follows:

	million tonnes		approximate mtce*
1983	115		195
1990	80	- 90	136 - 153
2000	50	- 90	85 - 153
2010	30	- 70	51 - 119
2020	10	- 25	17 - 43

* assuming 1 tonne oil = 1.7 tonnes coal

34

Natural gas production

Production of natural gas from the United Kingdom
sector of the North Sea has been on a plateau of
just below 4000 million cubic feet per day (14,000
million therms per year or the equivalent of about
56 million tonnes of coal per year) since 1978.
Falling output from the early discoveries in the
southern basin has been approximately offset by
supplies from northerly fields of both associated
gas (for example, through the Far North Liquids
and Associated Gas System) and non-associated gas
(the UK share of Frigg which is partly in the
Norwegian sector). Despite a continuing decline
in production from the early fields, there is
scope for expansion in UK gas output even with no
government policy change. More associated gas
will become available in the next few years.
Furthermore, exploration and development in the
southern basin are already increasing now that
direct sales to larger consumers are possible[10],
so that there is potential competition from other
gas purchasers for the British Gas Corporation.
Reports indicate that BGC has been offering much
higher prices than previously for gas from UK
fields[11]. We would expect the higher price policy
to continue, even though, in the absence of
freedom to export, UK gas producers are likely to
obtain lower prices than their Continental
counterparts.
   On our unchanged government policy
assumption, production may by 1990 be in the range
3500 to 4500 million cubic feet per day (mcfd),
equivalent to 51-66 mtce. After that time there
is considerable uncertainty. Output may by 2000
fall below 3000 mfcd. Thereafter some decline is
probable, although on a fairly optimistic view
even in 2010 natural gas output may be about the
same as in the early 1980s. The estimates we use
for the purposes of this chapter[12] are:

	million cubic feet per day	approximate mtce*
1983	3800	56
1990	3500 - 4500	51 - 66
2000	2700 - 4800	39 - 70
2010	2000 - 4000	29 - 58
2020	1500 - 3000	22 - 44

   * assuming 100 cubic feet per therm and 250
   therms per tonne of coal

Nuclear electricity production

Output of nuclear electricity in 1983 was the equivalent of 18 million tonnes of coal, having risen relatively little since the late 1960s when it was about 10 mtce a year. There have been operating problems with the early Magnox reactors and construction delays with the Advanced Gas Cooled Reactors (AGRs). Some expansion is in prospect but its scale is difficult to assess since it depends not only on overcoming technical problems but on the rate of growth of electricity demand and on the state of public attitudes to nuclear power.

Projections of nuclear capacity by governments and international organisations[13] have, in the past, been far too high. The most recent estimates published by the Department of Energy in its evidence to the Sizewell Inquiry seem to us still to be significantly higher than can reasonably be expected. In 1978 and 1979[14] the Department projected a 'maximum total installed nuclear capacity' of about 40 GW by 2000; although in its Sizewell evidence (Table 8) its estimates for 2000 have been much reduced to 13-28 GW, with 26-66 GW in 2010, the upper ends of its ranges (which assume $2\frac{1}{2}$ per cent a year growth in electricity sales) seem well in excess of what is likely.

Up to 1990, there is relatively little uncertainty about nuclear capacity. As the AGRs already under construction are completed, capacity should rise from about 7 GW in 1983 to 10-13 GW in 1990 (depending on whether Heysham II and Torness are then in service as they are scheduled to be). After 1990, however, uncertainty increases. On our unchanged government policy assumption we would expect construction of the Sizewell 'B' PWR to go ahead in the mid-1980s. We would then anticipate completion of at least one more PWR by 2000, and possibly as many as three more. If we take the probable minimum nuclear capacity in 2000 to include two PWRs (including Sizewell 'B') plus the AGRs now in operation or under construction and half the present Magnox capacity, nuclear capacity would then be 13 GW. If all the Magnox and AGR stations were still in service and four PWRs had been built, nuclear capacity would be about 17 GW[15]. Alternatively (but still within our unchanged government policy assumption), more

AGRs might be built instead of the PWRs: delays to the construction programme would probably then result and it is unlikely that output capacity would reach 17 GW.

By 2010 we assume all Magnox stations have been retired but all AGR stations are still operating. In addition, we assume a rather more substantial nuclear building programme beyond 2000 than in the 1990s (though much less than the Department of Energy assumes), which brings total nuclear capacity in 2010 to 20 to 30 GW. For 2020 our very speculative estimate is 20 to 50 GW. Our estimates[16] are therefore:

	GW output capacity	approximate mtce*
1983	7	18
1990	10 - 13	25 - 32
2000	13 - 17	32 - 42
2010	20 - 30	50 - 75
2020	20 - 50	50 - 125

* assuming 33% thermal efficiency, 65% load factor and 230 therms per tonne of coal

Hydro electric production

Hydro resources are severely limited by the geography of the United Kingdom, though 'natural' hydro is being supplemented by pumped storage schemes (as at Dinorwig) and there are a number of small-scale hydro schemes which may go ahead. It seems unlikely that, in the foreseeable future, hydro production will be much higher than in 1983 when it was equivalent to just under 2½ million tonnes of coal. We assume it to be in the range 2 to 4 mtce in 1990, 2000, 2010 and 2020.

Other energy sources

Several other forms of energy could eventually become substantial energy suppliers to United Kingdom consumers, although in the period we are considering they are likely to remain of minor importance. Income or 'renewable' sources of energy which do not draw on a capital stock (as does extraction of the fossil fuels and uranium) include solar power, wind, wave and tidal power and are potentially very large energy providers. 'Biofuels' - such as wood waste, straw, domestic

and industrial refuse - are coming into use as
fossil fuel prices increase. Geothermal power,
which is not a renewable, is also being used on a
small scale.

A detailed study of renewables made by the
Energy Technology Support Unit[17] and incorporated
in the Department of Energy's Sizewell evidence
gives estimates of about 2 to 6 mtce in 2000 and
about 6 to 21 mtce in 2010, excluding the Severn
Barrage which could provide electricity equivalent
to 5 million tonnes of coal. We have some
reservations about the upper end of the estimates
for 2010 (which are based on continuing
substantial real fossil fuel price increases after
2000) but we think it possible a Severn Barrage
could be operating by 2010. For the purpose of
this chapter we therefore use the following
figures which, up to 2010, are fairly close to the
Energy Department's Sizewell projections:

	mtce
1983	-
1990	½ - 1
2000	2 - 5
2010	5 - 20
2020	10 - 40

Self-sufficiency trends in the future

Our purpose in making the above general review of
possible energy production and consumption trends
is not to draw firm conclusions about the United
Kingdom's self-sufficiency ratio early next
century. Still less is it to recommend energy
import minimisation per se as a policy objective.
Our aim is merely to determine whether the country
is likely to remain close enough to self-
sufficiency for a self-sufficiency target to
appear attractive to policy-makers. As we have
seen (Chapter 2), in the past self-sufficiency
appears only to have figured as an objective of
policy when it seemed attainable at reasonable
cost. There would be little point in our
considering the costs and benefits of a self-
sufficiency aim if such a policy seemed outside
the range of practical politics.

It is, in fact, clear from the rather
speculative estimates given earlier in this
chapter that energy self-sufficiency may well
appear a feasible policy target for many years

yet. To illustrate, Table 3.1 gives a summary of the consumption and production estimates in the earlier part of this chapter. The table gives the approximate mid-points of the ranges of total fuel consumption and of production of each fuel: the sizes of the ranges are indicated by ± in each case. The range for total fuel production is less than the sum of the individual pluses and the individual minuses because there is likely to be some trade-off among the electricity generating fuels: for example, nuclear output towards the high end of its range is likely to mean coal output towards the low end of its range, and there may also be an inverse relationship between output of the renewables and nuclear production. Judgment has to be applied in estimating these trade-offs and so the range for total fuel production in each year should be regarded only as giving a very rough indication of the region in which total production is likely to lie. The self-sufficiency range, at the foot of the table, takes the low production and high production totals and divides each by the mid-point of the fuel consumption range[18].

Any attempt to draw precise conclusions from such speculative figures as those in Table 3.1 would be quite inappropriate. But in our view the data will allow the following inferences to be drawn (all assuming unchanged government policy):

- although UK fuel production can be expected to decline in the period we are considering, it will probably remain higher than in the 1960s and early 1970s when it was in the region of 170 to 200 mtce. Our estimates suggest that 25 or 30 years from now annual fuel production should be well in excess of 200 million tonnes and possibly over 350 million tonnes. Even in 2020 production might be between 200 and 300 million tonnes a year.
- much of the drop in UK fuel production may be expected before 2000 as output of both indigenous coal and North Sea oil is reduced. Between 2000 and 2010, except in the event of there being little new nuclear construction, indigenous fuel output may change little.
- from about 1990 onwards the self-sufficiency ratio will most probably fall, but in the early part of next century there is a good

chance it will be 0.6 or more - possibly
even still around 1. By 2010, however, the
ratio can be expected to fall well below 1:
our table shows a range of 0.6 - 0.9 in that
year, with 0.4 - 0.8 in 2020.
- although we have not in the table attempted
to estimate consumption of each fuel as well
as production, it is fairly clear that as
the energy self-sufficiency ratio declines
the consequent increase in imports will be
mainly in the form of oil and natural gas.
On our policy unchanged assumption, only
minimal coal imports will be allowed; in the
cases of nuclear, hydro and renewables, the
quantities produced will be consumed in the
UK (except to the extent that there is some
marginal electricity trade with the
Continent).

We should also remark that, if one accepts
the Department of Energy's future coal and nuclear
electricity estimates as given to the Sizewell
Inquiry, the future self-sufficiency ratio appears
considerably higher than on our estimates. In
2010, for example, the mid-point of the
Department's coal estimates (128 million tonnes)
is 35 million tonnes higher than the mid-point of
our estimates; a similar comparison for nuclear
shows the Department's mid-point 46 mtce above
ours. On their figures, the self-sufficiency
ratio might therefore seem likely to be in the
region of 1 even in 2010. Although we believe the
Energy Department estimates are still on the high
side and that they will probably be reduced in the
course of time, so long as they remain on the
table they will very likely influence both public
and government perceptions of self-sufficiency
trends and the feasibility of a self-sufficiency
policy.

A self-sufficiency policy for the future?

It seems, therefore, that for many years yet
energy self-sufficiency will appear to be a
feasible policy aim in the United Kingdom. In
such circumstances there may well be pressure on
governments (especially from indigenous energy
producers) to take steps to prolong self-
sufficiency. If it can be maintained at
apparently low economic cost and political

advantage can thereby be reaped, such a target is bound to seem appealing to governments, although there will inevitably be differences among the political parties in the signifance they attach to self-sufficiency and the ways they would try to achieve it.

To show that a policy of extending self-sufficiency is feasible is, however, quite different from showing that it would be socially beneficial. Some groups in society would benefit and politicians might gain votes from the beneficiaries, but the policy would not necessarily bring gains to the nation as a whole. There is evidently a popular belief that independence of foreigners for fuel supplies would, for security and perhaps other reasons, be advantageous. But one requires more than vague notions of public benefits if a policy with such far-reaching implications is to be pursued, and the costs need also to be counted.

If we take a self-sufficiency policy to mean aiming at a self-sufficiency ratio of 1 (which would not exclude some two-way trade in fuel, in which exports and imports were approximately equal), there appear to be four principal potential benefits:

- improved security from short-term disruptions in fuel supplies. Most people no doubt have particularly in mind the two oil 'shocks' of the 1970s and their effects; the belief evidently is that by keeping indigenous supplies equal to home consumption the effects of such events would be minimised.
- various long-term price-related gains. For instance, it could be that Britain would be able to reduce world energy prices by a self-sufficiency policy, or that the prices of indigenous fuels could be kept down, or that the country would be protected against unexpectedly high and damaging world energy prices.
- macro-economic advantages, such as higher real GDP, balance of payments gains, lower inflation and higher employment.
- benefits to distant generations because more energy resources might be available to them than if the country had not aimed at self-sufficiency.

Unchanged government policy

In Chapters 5 to 8 we discuss each of these potential advantages, but it will be helpful first in Chapter 4 to outline the various ways in which governments might approach a self-sufficiency policy.

1. Robinson and Marshall, Oil's Contribution to UK Self-Sufficiency, op.cit., Chap. 2, explains in more detail our 'policy unchanged' assumptions for the oil industry.

2. After this paper was written, the March 1984 Budget reduced the rate of Corporation Tax from 52 to 35 per cent by 1986-7 and removed first-year allowances for plant and machinery investment over the same period.

3. In What Future for British Coal?, op.cit., p. 47 we suggested a primary fuel demand range in the year 2000 of 400 to 450 mtce, though these estimates assumed 2 to 2½ per cent per annum real GDP growth and we described them as possibly on the high side; the Department of Energy's then current forecast was 445 to 510 mtce. The estimates we now give of 365 to 400 mtce in 2000 and 385-440 mtce in 2010 are a little below those in the cases (YU, YL, BU and BL) in the Energy Department's Proof of Evidence for the Sizewell 'B' Inquiry which assume a similar real GDP growth rate (1½ per cent) to ours (1 to 2 per cent). Other cases in the Sizewell Evidence fall well outside our fuel demand range but they assume economic growth rates which are higher or lower than ours.

4. What Future for British Coal? op.cit., especially pp. 69-71. Another study in this series by Louis Turner, Coal's Contribution to UK Self-Sufficiency, BIJEPP Paper No. 9, Heinemann, London, 1984 considers British coal policy. In Table 9 of the Turner study various forecasts of British coal demand are compared.

5. House of Commons, Second Report from the Select Committee on Energy, Session 1982-83, Pit Closures, HMSO, London, December 1982, paragraph 35. See also Robinson and Marshall, What Future for British Coal Policy?, Surrey Discussion Paper in Energy Economics, no. 14, May 1983.

6. Financial Times, European Energy Report, 1 April 1983, p. 13.

7. Proof of Evidence for the Sizewell 'B' Inquiry, op.cit., Tables C and D. We presume that the Department is assuming only small coal imports and exports so that UK production would be similar to UK consumption of coal.

8. See What Future for British Coal Policy?, op.cit., Turner, op.cit., and Monopolies and Mergers Commission, op.cit.

9.   Robinson and Marshall, Oil's Contribution to UK Self-Sufficiency, op.cit., Chap. 2.

10.   Under the Oil and Gas (Enterprise) Act of 1982.

11.   See, for example,'British Gas beats off ICI', The Financial Times, 19 September 1983, where it is reported that British Gas offered 22 to 23 pence per therm for gas from three Hamilton Brothers fields.

12.   Our estimates are the same as those used by Jonathan Stern in Gas's Contribution to UK Self-Sufficiency, Heinemann, London, 1984, except that the upper end of our range is rather higher in 1990 (4500 instead of 3900 million cubic feet per day).   A more optimistic view of future supplies has been suggested by British Petroleum. See 'BP makes waves over North Sea gas', The Financial Times, 6 May 1983.

13.   For some comparisons of nuclear capacity projections made at different times see OECD, Nuclear Energy and its Fuel Cycle: Prospects to 2025, Paris, 1982, especially Table IV.5.

14.   Energy Policy: A Consultative Document, op.cit., paragraph 10.18, and Energy Projections 1979, op.cit., p. 7.

15.   The estimate of 13-17 GW nuclear capacity in 2000 is at the lower end of the range we suggested in 1981 of 15-25 GW.   The 'nuclear delays' scenario we then used had 15 GW of nuclear capacity in 2000.   See What Future for British Coal?, op.cit.,especially pp. 95-6.

16.   In Electricity's Contribution to UK Self-Sufficiency, Heinemann, London, 1984, Eden and Evans give possible ranges of future nuclear capacity.   Their 'central trend' ranges for 2000 (13-19 GW) and 2020 (16-56 GW) are similar to, though slightly wider than, ours.

17.   ETSU, Contribution of Renewable Energy Technologies to Future Energy Requirements, Report R14, HMSO, London, 14 January 1983.

18.   A wider self-sufficiency range would, of course, be obtained if low production was divided by high consumption and vice versa.   The method we use here is consistent with that used in Oil's Contribution to UK Self-Sufficiency, op.cit.

Table 3.1: Primary fuel consumption and production estimates

mtce

	1983 Actual	1990	2000	2010	2020
			------Estimated------		
FUEL CONSUMPTION	328	353±8	383±18	413±28	445±40
FUEL PRODUCTION					
Coal	119	105±10	93±18	93±18	87±18
Oil	195	145±8	119±34	85±34	30±13
Natural gas	56	59±8	55±15	44±15	33±11
Nuclear	18	29±4	37±5	63±13	88±38
Hydro	2	3±1	3±1	3±1	3±1
Renewables	–	1±1	4±2	13±8	25±15
TOTAL	390	342±30	311±65	301±70	266±75
SELF-SUFFICIENCY RATIO*	1.19	0.9-1.1	0.6-1.0	0.6-0.9	0.4-0.8

* for 1990 onwards the extremes of the ranges are, respectively, low production and high production, each divided by the mid-point of the consumption range.

Note: the basis for this table is explained on page 38.

45

Chapter Four

APPROACHES TO A SELF-SUFFICIENCY POLICY

There are three broad avenues of approach open to a government aiming at energy self-sufficiency - output deferral, repletion and demand-side conservation.

Output deferral

If the country concerned has an energy export surplus (a self-sufficiency ratio in excess of one), the government could defer some energy output to a later period when there would otherwise have been net imports of energy. In other words, any 'hump' of energy production could be flattened so that production would be equated with consumption for as long a period as possible. Most Western industrial countries do not have the option of output deferral because they would embark on any attempt at energy self-sufficiency as net importers. Britain, however, is in the unusual situation of being able to defer some energy production to prolong self-sufficiency should it so choose since, as explained in Chapter 1, it is now a substantial net exporter. In 1983 its energy self-sufficiency ratio was about 1.2, and the ratio is likely to remain above one for some years yet if government policy remains unchanged. Thus a British government embarking in the mid-1980s on a policy of extending self-sufficiency would presumably, as its first act, seek means of reducing indigenous production into line with home consumption.

In practice, oil production is much more likely to be regulated than production of other forms of energy. The self-sufficiency ratio for oil alone was about 1.6 in 1983, so that there was

a big surplus of output over home consumption, and
as we have shown in another study in this series[1],
this surplus can be expected to persist at least
into the early 1990s and possibly for much longer
(with government policy unchanged).

Alternatively, energy self-sufficiency could
be extended by considerably increasing imports of
coal and natural gas at the expense of home
production so as to offset oil exports: in that
way, to the extent it was technically feasible,
some indigenous coal and gas production could be
held back for the future. But such a policy does
not seem probable in the near future. Coal
exports and imports are only a few million tonnes
a year so there is already approximate
self-sufficiency in that market, largely as a
result of a government policy of limiting
imports. The rundown in coal production which is
already in progress is causing enough social and
political difficulties and it is hardly likely
that governments would add to those in the 1980s
by increasing coal imports merely to allow oil
exports to continue for a period. In the case of
gas, about twenty-five per cent of consumption is
already supplied by imports. Any action taken now
to increase imports (from Norway, Holland or the
Soviet Union, for instance) would not bring new
supplies until the late 1980s, or early 1990s, by
which time oil production would be well past its
peak and the energy self-sufficiency ratio might,
with unchanged policy, have reverted to around one
(see Chapter 3).

Another reason for believing that oil
production would be the most likely candidate for
cutbacks under a deferral policy in the 1980s and
1990s is that the machinery for depletion controls
already exists. It would be possible for crude
oil exports to be regulated by quota or by
deliberate pricing above the world level. More
probable though, would be the use of the
regulatory mechanism contained in the Petroleum
and Submarine Pipelines Act of 1975[2] which would
not lead to the same international complications
(for instance, conflict with EEC rules and
possible retaliation from other countries) as
would explicit controls on exports. Present
government assurances on the use of production
restrictions expire at the end of 1984 so it would
be possible to apply controls from early 1985.

We do not discuss in any detail here the
consequences of a policy of deferring oil output

47

to achieve self-sufficiency. As we have explained
at length elsewhere[3], there would be immense
complications in such a policy and considerable
costs could arise which need to be set against
potential benefits. The present value of United
Kingdom oil reserves would probably be depressed;
the oil companies' willingness to invest would
most likely be diminished, so that governments
wishing to avoid a reduction in eventually
recovered oil reserves would almost certainly have
to give tax concessions or some other incentive to
the companies; it would be very hard for
governments to know how much production to defer
and for how long; and there would be increased
politicisation of the oil market.

Repletion

The second approach to self-sufficiency is by
means of 'repletion'[4] - increasing the total
amount of energy produced in the United Kingdom in
some time period, compared with what it would have
been with unchanged policy.
    Repletion itself can take two forms. One is
the temporary expedient of bringing energy
production forward: by accelerating the rate of
depletion of fossil fuel reserves self-sufficiency
could be maintained for a period, though at the
expense of lower production later. The other, and
probably more important, form of repletion aims at
increasing the total amount of energy eventually
produced in the UK.
    For example, a government intent on the
second form of repletion could encourage higher
recovery rates from coal, oil and natural gas
reserves which would in any case have been
exploited, and it could bring into production
fossil fuel reserves which otherwise would not
have been developed at all. Renewable energy
resources (such as wind, solar and possibly tidal
and wave power) could be exploited earlier and in
larger quantities than would otherwise have been
the case. An enhanced nuclear programme is
another option in a repletion strategy. There may
be a sizeable import content in a nuclear
programme, so that it is not clearly an
'indigenous' source of energy[5]. Nevertheless,
commissioning more nuclear stations would conserve
some fossil fuel resources for the future, so that
this form of repletion would also have production-
deferring effects.

Constraints would be imposed on the form of any repletion programme because different sources of energy are imperfect substitutes one for another. As we have seen (Chapter 3), in the absence of a self-sufficiency policy it is imports of oil and gas which are most likely to rise as home demand outruns indigenous supplies. Thus a repletion programme directed primarily at stimulating output of nuclear electricity, renewables and coal would not directly meet consumers' needs for liquid and gaseous fuels (though in the long run it might be possible to gasify and liquefy coal economically).

Except to the extent that it involved accelerating production, a repletion policy would require two kinds of action by government. First, there would be enabling measures, such as opening up larger areas of the country (onshore and offshore) for fossil fuel exploration in the hope that more discoveries would be made and more energy resouces would be developed. Second, this form of repletion would involve steps to increase the attractiveness of energy production of all kinds. As far as private companies were concerned, the main need would be to increase after-tax profitability (for example, by reducing tax rates, providing subsidies, or increasing prices) so that there would be greater willingness to exploit new finds, to extract a greater proportion of known reserves, and to invest in new forms of energy production. Since a considerable part of the UK energy sector is nationalised and since public corporations which make large profits are frequently subject to criticism, different forms of incentives might need to be devised for the nationalised corporations.

Just as production deferral would involve costs, so there would be costs in a repletion strategy arising from greater investment of resources in repletion measures than there would be with policy unchanged, and from a more politicised energy market. We discuss some of these costs in principle at the end of this chapter.

Conservation

Finally, there is an approach to self-sufficiency from the demand side rather than the supply side. As a complement to or a substitute for output

49

deferral and repletion, governments could deliberately try to reduce the demand for energy. That is, for any given level of output in the economy they could try to bring about lower energy use by imposing taxes on consumption, by giving subsidies for conservation, or possibly by rationing supplies of energy. Rationing could be direct or indirect; it could, for example, take the form of speed limits imposed for 'energy efficiency' reasons. This kind of demand-side conservation would incur costs similar in nature to those we have mentioned in connection with deferral and repletion policies. In addition, social control costs could arise from the imposition of non-price rationing.

The interdependence of deferral, repletion and conservation

In Britain, starting as it does with an energy export surplus, it would apparently be possible to extend self-sufficiency, first by deferring energy (principally oil) output and then by repletion and demand-side conservation measures. It should, however, be pointed out that there may be conflicts between the three avenues of approach. For example, because of the long time lags in bringing new energy production and some conservation schemes to fruition, it would be necessary to implement repletion and conservation measures at the same time that output was being deferred. Consequently, private companies and nationalised corporations which made investments under a repletion programme might find that, because of energy conservation and output deferral schemes, they had to 'shut in' production for several years. If such circumstances were foreseen, the incentive to invest would inevitably be diminished and governments might find that compensating subsidies were required.

The principle of extending self-sufficiency

It is not the purpose of this study to give detailed accounts of self-sufficiency policies for particular fuels. That is the function of the other volumes of this series. Our prime concern is with issues of principle with respect to energy self-sufficiency policies in general.

From what we have said above, it should be clear that, whichever approach to self-sufficiency is taken, the principle is essentially the same. It is a matter of 'over-investing', in the sense of channelling more investment in a particular direction than there would be with unchanged government policy. For example, production deferral is a policy of more investment in energy resources in the ground than would otherwise occur: leaving fossil fuel reserves in the ground to be produced later rather than extracting them now is just as much an investment as building a new factory and equipping it with machinery. Similarly, repletion means investing more in exploration for fossil fuels, development of reserves, and enhanced recovery schemes than there would be with unchanged policy: it can also mean greater investment in renewable energy sources and nuclear power. Finally, demand-side conservation means additional investment to reduce the consumption of energy per unit of output.

By 'over-investing' in resources in the ground, or in repletion, or in demand-side conservation, society incurs the opportunity costs of not employing its resources in other ways. There may also be costs associated with increased government control of the energy market and other side-effects of a self-sufficiency policy.

Whether or not a policy designed to achieve self-sufficiency is likely to be socially beneficial depends on the size of these costs (suitably discounted) and on the extent of any likely discounted benefits. 'Over-investment' might, for instance, be justified if private companies were using discount rates in evaluating energy projects which were higher than society would wish to use. Companies would, in such circumstances, invest too little in resources in the ground, in finding and developing new sources of energy production, and in demand-side conservation projects. A social gain could therefore result if investment could be increased to the 'correct' level. Similarly, it is possible that there are social benefits attached to indigenous energy production which mean that the international market price of such energy is less than its social value, and production is therefore less than society would wish whereas demand is greater. Private producers cannot, for instance,

51

capture all the benefits of providing security of supply (which has some of the attributes of a 'public good'[6]) and so they may not supply all the security society would like.

In the next four chapters of this study we analyse the potential benefits of an energy self-sufficiency policy, concentrating on those which were identified at the end of Chapter 3.

1.   Robinson   and   Marshall,   *Oil's Contribution to UK Self-Sufficiency*, op.cit., especially chaps. 2 and 4.

2.   The Act provides that the Secretary of State for Energy can approve, modify or reject plans submitted by producers which must specify their intended capital investment and propose maximum and minimum annual production rates for oil and gas.

3.   *Oil's   Contribution   to   UK   Self-Sufficiency*, especially chaps. 3-6.

4.   The term seems first to have been used in House of Commons Select Committee on Energy, Third Report, Session 1981-2, *North Sea Oil Depletion Policy*, para. 95.

5.   Uranium has to be imported into the UK and there are also likely to be imports of technology and equipment, depending on the reactor type.   All forms of energy production in the UK are likely to require some imports.   North Sea oil production, for instance, involves the purchase of some overseas equipment and services and an outflow of profits abroad.

6.   The reason why the   market will tend to under-value security of supply is that security has some of the characteristics of a 'public good'.   Supply of a pure public good would benefit all members of society whether they paid for it or not, and private producers would therefore have no incentive to provide the good since they could not appropriate the benefits by charging for it.   In practice,   individuals   and   organisations   can provide some security for themselves and retain the benefits (for example, by holding excess fuel stocks) but some of the benefits will spill over to others.

Chapter Five

SELF-SUFFICIENCY AND SECURITY OF SUPPLY

Distinguishing self-sufficiency from security of supply

The aim which most often appears to be implicitly associated with an energy self-sufficiency policy is an improvement in the nation's security of energy supplies. 'Security of supply' is itself an imprecise term since no energy form and no source of supply can offer absolute security. We define it to mean relative freedom from sudden physical shortages and any resultant short-term price increases which disrupt the economic and social life of the country. Improving security of supply therefore means reducing the number of such disruptions and the impact on society of any which still occur. A complication is that threats to interrupt supplies may be as significant in their effects as interruptions themselves.

Advocates of a self-sufficiency policy seem to assume that domestic damage from supply disruption and threats to supplies would be minimised by such a policy. Indeed, in popular discussion security-maximising and import-minimising policies are sometimes regarded as virtually identical. Presumably that is because, to many people, indigenous supplies appear to be inherently more 'secure' than imports. However, experience tells us that indigenous supplies are also prone to interruptions, for instance, because of industrial action, civil disorder or accidents. We consider below the likely effects of a self-sufficiency policy on the security of indigenous supplies and on the cost of coping with indigenous supply emergencies. Then we examine self-sufficiency in relation to the likely domestic consequences of international fuel market disruptions.

Self-sufficiency and indigenous energy supplies

If the government is explicitly committed to a policy of energy self-sufficiency, any interruption to indigenous supplies will be potentially more damaging than it would be to an import-dependent country, because a greater proportion of supplies will be affected. However, not only may the impact of an indigenous supply interruption be greater but the probability of interruptions or threats of interruptions increases because of the greater leverage of indigenous energy industries and associated groups.

The more concentrated are indigenous energy supplies in the hands of monopolistic private companies, public corporations or labour unions, the greater is the security threat likely to be, and the more anxious may governments be to seek an early settlement of disputes, especially since, under a self-sufficiency policy, government will inevitably be seen as primarily responsible for any energy supply problems. The short-term costs to the nation from large-scale fuel supply cuts will be both large and visible. Even the threat of cuts is costly in that it creates uncertainty, causes distress and leads to precautionary actions by consumers, such as buying in extra supplies. The costs of 'giving-in' - covered by taxpayers, shareholders, or fuel consumers in higher prices - are thinly spread, less obvious and difficult to quantify. It is hard to know whether the result of an energy self-sufficiency policy will necessarily be more indigenous supply interruptions. But, in our view, increased threats of interruptions are likely and may result in fuel producers gaining at other people's expense.

As an example of the possible result of a self-sufficiency policy on security of supply, one can refer to the recent history of coal in Britain[1]. In the 1970s imported oil supplies were perceived as insecure and rising oil prices provided the 'headroom' for wages, other costs and prices to rise in British coal mining. At the same time, statements of support by governments, endorsement of the NCB's Plan for Coal and increasing subsidisation by the government gave the employees of the coal industry the impression that they were in an organisation of increasing importance to the nation. Since it was generally believed that no significant volume of coal imports would be allowed, Britain had something close to a self-sufficiency policy for coal. The evident increased bargaining strength of the coal industry's labour force resulted in two serious industrial disputes in the early 1970s. In the winter of 1971/72 there was an overtime ban followed by a strike and the 'Wilberforce' pay settlement. Then in 1973/74, at a time when oil supplies were already short, there was another overtime ban and subsequently a particularly disruptive strike; the Conservatives lost a General Election apparently because they did not 'give-in' and there was another substantial pay increase after the return of a Labour government.

For a number of years thereafter no serious supply interruptions occurred but there were frequent threats of interruptions which had the effects mentioned above. Precautionary actions were taken by coal consumers; the Central Electricity Generating Board in particular frequently had to incur the costs of increasing its stocks of coal, chemicals and other vital materials and using more oil because of threatened coal strikes. There were also signs that, despite a large price differential in coal's favour, consumers were wary of switching from oil to coal, on security of supply grounds. Governments, which evidently feared that they might suffer the same fate as the Conservatives in February 1974, were unwilling in the rest of the 1970s and early 1980s to face the consequences of more coal strikes. The most notable example of the powerful effects of threatened disruptions occurred in February 1981, when the Conservative government, concerned at the gathering momentum of unofficial miners' strikes, radically changed the policy it had only just instituted of reducing subsidies for the industry. Instead, it increased aid for coal mining and severely restricted imports which by then were beginning to enter the British market in increasing amounts (see Chapter 2). In our view, one of the most important costs of coal policy in that period was the reduction in security arising from increased monopolisation of the fuel market by indigenous producers. The perceived impact on total fuel supplies of interruptions in indigenous coal supply was increased by government import-minimising policy, and, not surprisingly, threats to interrupt coal supply were frequent and costly for taxpayers and fuel consumers.

One result of this period in which the monopoly power of the coal industry was enhanced by government action was that a serious and costly confrontation eventually occurred. By the latter part of 1983, over-production of coal led to excessive stocks and it became obvious that the coal industry's output targets for the 1980s and 1990s were greatly inflated[2]. Disappointed expectations in a labour force which had been led to believe it was in an expanding industry caused considerable bitterness and a desire to use its power to withhold supplies. From the autumn of 1983, the miners began an overtime ban in support of a pay claim. Then, in March 1984, area strikes (except in Nottinghamshire) began against the Coal Board's pit closure programme. At the time of writing (August 1984) the strikes continued, though with a very slow drift back to work. The costs of the dispute were by then very considerable. Precautionary action by consumers, and particularly by the Central Electricity Generating Board[3] (which incurred heavy costs in building up excess stocks of coal and other materials and burning expensive oil so as to economise on coal usage), and costly policing of the dispute mitigated some of its effects. Nevertheless, Britain suffered serious social, political and managerial disruption in a dispute which gave the clearest possible demonstration of how pursuing self-sufficiency can make energy supplies less secure.

Concentration of energy supplies, whether or not in indigenous hands, can also increase the scope for disruptive action by individuals and groups outside the fuel industries themselves. For example, terrorist activity is, ceteris paribus, more of a threat the fewer are a country's fuel supply sources. Supplies whose security is most important to the nation are the most probable targets, as are those sources where there could be chain effects between plants - for example, where sabotage endangers the workers in an industry and there are sympathetic stoppages in other plants, or where sabotage creates a public outcry for shut down of similar or associated plant. Accidents can, of course, similarly threaten supplies. It is possible, for instance, that major supply difficulties would arise following an accident to a nuclear establishment or to nuclear waste during transportation (perhaps even if such an event occurred in another country), if Britain was heavily dependent on indigenous nuclear-generated electricity.

Security of supply

Avoiding indigenous supply disruptions

To some extent Britain could avoid the adverse
effects on security of an energy self-sufficiency
policy, whilst still maintaining that policy.
Emergency provisions such as stockpiling and spare
capacity (see next section) may themselves help to
deter threats to supplies and actual disruptions,
but other options are also available. For
example, specific protection from sabotage and
accident could take the form of strict internal
and external security regulations, although such
measures, costly in themselves, can have important
indirect costs in the creation of oppressive
régimes in which to work and live. The threat to
security from industrial disputes in monopolised
industries could be lessened by 'no strike'
employment contracts but, in addition to the
direct costs of such measures, indirect costs
would be likely to arise if other groups in
society argued the case for similar treatment.
    The security problem we have identified is a
consequence of the concentration of power in
indigenous energy and associated industries. A
policy of deliberately dispersing power would
therefore probably offer certain security
advantages. If, for instance, the fuel sector was
relatively free from direct government influence,
was diversified by fuel, by suppliers and by plant
design, and had local labour bargaining,it would
be likely to provide greater security of supply
than if it were dominated by a few organisations.
The extent to which such diversification would be
effective in preventing national disruption would
depend on the substitutability of energy sources
and 'on the extent to which fuel from one location
and one supplier could be substituted for the same
fuel from another. It would also depend on the
absence of collusion between employers and between
unions. Whether greater diversification by fuel,
suppliers and plant, for security of supply
reasons, increased the cost of domestic energy
would depend on economies of scale and the size of
the domestic market.
    Energy imports,provided they are diversified
by fuel and by source, seem to us to be a
particularly important security-enhancing measure
rather than the threat to security which they are
often assumed to be. Even though imports from any
one source may well be vulnerable, the factors
precipitating import supply disruptions and the

timing of such disruptions from different sources
are unlikely to coincide. Nor are they likely to
be coincident with indigenous supply problems;
indeed, both regular supplies of imported energy
and the prospect of increasing imports in an
emergency may help to deter threats from domestic
fuel suppliers. A self-sufficiency policy which
allowed a balanced trade in exports and imports
would weaken this deterrence effect; it would
impede the flow of imports competitive with
indigenous supplies and it would almost certainly
fail to provide the port and transportation
facilities needed to increase imports of fuel
significantly and to import specific fuels in an
emergency. An explicit policy of eliminating all
trade in fuels would be worse; by raising a
political barrier to fuel imports on a regular or
irregular basis, it would effectively remove the
deterrence effect.

We turn now to a discussion of possible
measures to cope with widespread domestic supply
cuts with a self-sufficiency policy in operation.
In general, we assume that imports are not
available, though we point out in various places
how energy imports could help.

Emergency measures

In theory, an 'optimal' level of emergency
provision ought to balance the expected marginal
costs of emergency measures - such as fuel
stockpiling and spare productive capacity - with
the expected marginal benefits. Such calculations,
however, are bound to be highly subjective.
Calculating the expected benefits curve in
particular is extremely difficult, involving
estimates of the size, duration and frequency of
prospective supply interruptions and of their
economic effects, because of limited substitution
possibilities. A major difficulty is that costs
would be social as well as economic and thus only
partly captured in lost GNP calculations (which
would themselves be only rough approximations).

Moreover, planning for supply disruptions
cannot be geared just to loss of output since,
even with a small overall cut, the demand side
reaction may be perverse[4] and may thus accentuate
supply problems, especially when total reliance is
placed on domestic resources. Normally, domestic
supply loss could be expected to increase prices

and decrease demand. Although there might be some stockbuilding for a time, with free-trading policies higher prices would soon attract international re-routing of energy supplies; thus both demand and supply responses would help to prevent the crisis from escalating. Without imports, expectations might well be formed that a domestic crisis would worsen before it became better: thus hoarding would be encouraged with a consequent amplified rise in price. Emergency preparedness for a supply crisis must therefore take account not only of the elasticity of the demand curve but also of a possible shift in the demand curve to the right. A bigger shift would be likely with fuel self-sufficiency in operation than without it.

One question which arises when considering safeguards against supply emergencies is whether the government needs to be involved in precautionary arrangements. Private precautions to cope with a sudden supply emergency could include, for example, building individual user stockpiles, installing emergency generating capacity, investing in dual-firing, or perhaps using an insurance market. Such arrangements would help but would not be entirely reliable means of emergency provision, whether or not there were imports, for the following reasons.

First, under-investment is likely to occur partly because of a classic 'free-rider' problem; security provision is to some extent a 'public good' whose benefits cannot entirely be appropriated by private suppliers[5]. The expectation that, in an emergency, governments might by-pass market mechanisms for distributing available supplies (for instance, seizing private stocks) would further encourage private under-investment, as would the general belief that government 'will provide' in an emergency. In theory at least, with well-developed markets in risk, it would be possible to insure against supply loss. In practice, however, even were such a market to operate widely, the service would probably be perceived as prohibitively costly, incorporating a high risk premium and high running costs. It would be impossible to forecast future liability, claims would be bunched, and storing energy or maintaining spare capacity would themselves be expensive. A self-sufficiency policy would, for reasons discussed earlier, probably exacerbate the problems and raise the costs.

Second, not only would market solutions tend to under-provide for fuel emergencies, they might be regarded as socially unacceptable during crisis situations. That is because they embody an implicit collective judgement that the risk-averse, those better informed of likely risks, and those able to afford private provision or insurance should be secure against energy shortages while the risk-takers, the ill-informed and the poor should not.

The 'public good' properties of provision against fuel supply cuts suggest government responsibility for deciding the 'correct' level of provision against scarcity in an emergency, based perhaps on an imperfect cost/benefit analysis or on the adoption of a worst-case policy. Furthermore, it can be argued that a government is responsible for ensuring that the 'correct' level is attained by the least-cost route (whether by encouraging further private provision, by public provision or by some combination of the two) and the least-cost means (for instance, stockpiling or maintaining spare capacity). In addition, because of distributional conflicts that are likely to arise if fuel becomes suddenly scarce and expensive, a government may be involved in an explicit decision about how scarce emergency supplies are to be rationed.

A useful and potentially cost-effective precaution in a domestic fuel emergency would be a fund of money, financed from taxation or insurance premiums, with which to purchase imports to alleviate the crisis. Such a fund could be used to supplement and to a certain extent replace other forms of emergency provision; instead of the country incurring storage or maintenance costs, the fund would earn interest in the interim between emergencies. There is no reason to believe that bought-in supplies would be particularly expensive unless a domestic fuel emergency coincided with an international crisis. Imports would also add flexibility to emergency provision, the amount of extra imports being tailored to the particular domestic emergency. Without such flexibility, the problems of assessing the level of emergency preparedness and the forms it should take become formidable, especially because of the likely bigger rightward shift of the demand curve in a domestic crisis in which imports are not available.

Security of supply

If domestic fuel emergencies arose because of
industrial disputes, attempts could well be made
to stop imports from entering the country. To do
so would require considerable solidarity between
different groups of workers, however, and would be
more difficult the greater the diversity of
imports in terms of types of fuel, suppliers and
points of entry. For instance, during the 1984
coal strike attempts to ban coal imports had
limited success but increased use of imported fuel
oil helped the power industry to cope with the
disruption.
    Rationing costs would also be likely to
increase in the event of a domestic emergency
which arose under a policy of self-sufficiency.
In such circumstances it is more likely that the
crisis would be regarded as politically-created
and that the government and not the market would b
perceived as responsible for its solution. Hence
market distribution of the scarce energy resources
(modified by special provision for the needy) is
less likely to be a viable option than in a
'market'-created situation. Widespread political
choices concerning a hierarchy of 'deserving'
cases, bureaucratic allocation procedures and the
reaction these kinds of arrangements are likely to
engender in consumers (some for instance will
overstate their 'needs' whereas others would not
claim their full entitlement) are all likely
further to increase the real cost of a domestic
energy crisis.
    We would conclude on emergency provision
that, though the government needs to be involved
in emergency measures to cope with any possible
domestic energy supply emergency, its task is
likely to be unnecessarily difficult and costly if
it is at the same time operating an energy
self-sufficiency policy.

Self-sufficiency and the world energy market

So far we have been concerned with disruptions to
indigenous supplies. We now consider whether an
energy self-sufficiency policy would reduce the
impact of supply interruptions emanating from
overseas and would give Britain greater freedom
for unilateral action and a reduced need for
international co-ordination of policies to promote
security.

Clearly it is reasonable to expect that energy imports will on occasions be subject to sudden supply disruptions or threats of disruption. Accidents may occur or there may be deliberate attempts to restrict supplies. Energy interdependence, because it can be a positive sum game, may reduce conflicts of interest among countries, just as a prospering domestic energy industry can provide both higher wages and lower prices. But even when all parties gain in absolute terms, there is still considerable room for dispute about the distribution of such gains, whether between workers and consumers at home or internationally between exporters and importers of energy. When energy markets are depressed, the potential for strife is even greater. A cyclical international market is therefore in itself a threat to security, especially because in some countries energy revenues form a large part of the total GNP. Even small international price decreases may in those circumstances lead to serious internal strains, disputes between suppliers over market share, and attempts at supply-side fine-tuning, all of which may bring about a sudden loss of output and rising and erratic market prices. Threats to imported supplies are also possible from outside the international energy market itself, from instability within one country or from wars between countries as is obvious from the recent history of the Middle East.

Thus it is to be expected that there will be occasional supply disruptions originating overseas. Imported coal supplies might be reduced by political problems in Poland or South Africa or by strikes in Australia or the United States; gas imports might be affected because the Russians decide for military reasons to pump less gas through their pipelines to the West or because the Algerians are holding out for higher prices; and imports of oil might be cut because of an Arab oil embargo, because of a revolution in a Middle East producing country or because the Strait of Hormuz is closed in an escalation of the Gulf War. Everyone would like to be free from the effects of such disruptive events, and many people would like the United Kingdom to be able to pursue an energy policy which suits its own circumstances, regardless of what is happening in the rest of the world. But the point at issue is not simply whether one would like to avoid disturbances and constraints arising abroad. The question is whether it is actually likely that, by a self-sufficiency policy, the effects of overseas disruptions of energy supplies could be avoided. Having dealt with that question, we can then judge what benefits there might be left to set against the security costs of self-sufficiency mentioned in the earlier part of this chapter.

Avoiding the effects of overseas supply disruptions?

Contrary to popular belief, in the absence of energy self-sufficiency, a deliberate attempt by other countries to cut off Britain's fuel imports would not necessarily be very damaging, as evidenced by the limited effects of the attempted embargoes of the United States and the Netherlands in 1973. If energy became suddenly more scarce in one country or a few countries because of loss of supplies, then prices in those countries would rise relatively, and the profit motive in an international energy market would in time bring about a re-distribution of available resources and would even out the supply loss and the price rise.

However, it is also true that, even with an energy self-sufficiency policy, Britain would not be free from harm caused by short-term disruption in other parts of the international market, although the effects would be indirect rather than specifically affecting fuel supplies. Just as a supply loss in one part of the domestic energy market would be imperfectly generalised to the rest of the energy industry and eventually to the whole of the domestic economy - the extent depending on substitutability between fuels and between energy and other factors of production - so too would a cutback in the form of internationally traded energy affect the whole international energy market and the world economy.

Britain would feel the impact of these repercussions on the world economy, since its own trading position would eventually be affected. That would be so even if it were possible to maintain a ban on net energy exports and to hold domestic prices below the increased international levels, without retaliation from trading partners and without repercussions on the exchange rate, both of which seem unlikely. Furthermore, if international energy markets were disrupted due to an accident with a specific technology - for instance, a particular type of nuclear reactor - then the impact on the domestic economy could be direct as well as indirect since it could force a shutdown of some indigenous energy supplies.

Probably the most economically self-interested response to an international energy market emergency for a country like Britain with substantial domestic energy resources would be to raise domestic prices to world levels and export any surplus energy at world market prices. Such a response would lessen the chances of retaliatory threats and of erratic exchange rate movements; it would also ensure that scarce energy resources were used in their highest value uses, thus minimising the general economic impact of the supply disruption. However, if an energy self-sufficiency policy were in operation, such a deviation would probably be politically impossible. The costs at home would be immediate and obvious, whereas the gains would be spread over a longer period and would be less apparent to the public. Moreover, such a policy change might seem inexplicable to the electorate, since immunity from sudden cutbacks in demand and increased fuel prices arising from events abroad would be perceived as a basic reason for the adoption of energy self-sufficiency in the first place.

For the reasons we have given, it is clear that a policy of energy self-sufficiency would not free the UK from all the repercussions of international energy market disturbances. Nor is it likely that Britain could pursue independent energy policies and avoid participating in international efforts to promote security. Indeed, if a policy of energy self-sufficiency were adopted, the UK would have self-interested reasons to promote secure international supplies of energy, not only to minimise damage to the world economic order but also to lessen the chance of retaliation for its own energy-independent trading stance. Such co-operation would not be costless and might take the form, for instance, of encouraging competition in world energy markets by transfer of technology to potential producers, and negotiating for international agreements of co-operation with present producers, as well as participation in international emergency measures to cope with a sudden international supply shock.

Security of supply

The only advantage we can see of being self-sufficient in the event of an overseas supply disruption is in escaping the possibly very damaging immediate economic and social effects of a cut-off specifically directed at the UK's own energy imports. If the UK were not energy self-sufficient, the higher the proportion of its total energy consumption that was cut off from abroad, the more dramatic would such immediate effects be before the international trade in energy came to the rescue by diverting supplies to the UK. Both diversified sources of imports and indigenous supplies would be valuable in lessening the chances of embargo threats and reducing the damage caused by an actual cut-off of supplies. There is, however, the danger, which to some extent can be countered by diversifying supply sources, that domestic industrial disputes will be aligned to import disruptions (as in the case of the 1973 miners' strike) in an attempt to maximise the benefits to the indigenous workers concerned.

Strategic energy policy[6]

Another aspect of energy supply security is the needs of national defence ('strategic energy policy'). National defence is intended to 'buy' protection from the occurrence of international conflict and a greater probability of national survival in the event of war. Thus, just as civil energy security should take account of both threats and actual disruptions to supply, so too should strategic energy policy consider likely energy-related threats to international political order, as well as energy requirements in the event of UK involvement in an international conflict. Whilst the availability of indigenous energy supplies is likely to be important for strategic reasons, it is doubtful whether maintaining self-sufficiency for as long as possible would lessen the possibility of armed conflict, or necessarily promote continuity of essential supplies in an actual emergency.

Orthodox economic analysis stresses the substantial contribution of international trade to world prosperity and peace because it binds nations together. Thus, whilst the international pursuit of political power and prestige tends to be 'zero-sum' in that one country (or group of countries) can gain at others' expense,

66

international economic activity can generate a surplus from which all parties can gain in terms of increased economic welfare.

Conflict nevertheless occurs in economic relations among countries. Concentration of economic power in the hands of producers or consumers can reduce the overall gains from trade and redistribute what remains in favour of the monopolist or monopsonist. For instance, the large oil price increases in the 1970s redistributed gains away from importers to the oil exporters. There is something to be said in such circumstances for concerted action by importers in an attempt to recapture a portion of welfare 'lost' to the producers (see Chapter 6). But elimination rather than tactical adjustment of the energy trade would remove the long-term economic gains to both producers and consumers and, of more relevance to strategic energy policy, would also remove the international political restraint that such gains engender. International concentrations of economic power are potentially dangerous in that economic manoeuvring over distribution of the gains from trade may result in political rather than economic retaliation, and include the use of force. Moves which diversify the international energy market may therefore be both economically advantageous and peace-enhancing.

Concentrations of economic power, coupled to the costliness of making major economic adjustments quickly, can also render sudden interruptions to trade (threatened or actual) a powerful political weapon. A primary strategic concern is to prevent a short-term disruption to imported supplies being used for political ends. A possible course of action to prevent this from happening is military deterrence. For example, the threat to oil security seems to be a principal justification for the creation of the USA's Rapid Deployment Force. However, although such forces may help deter supply disruption from abroad, a more cost-effective policy may be the kind of emergency provisions outlined earlier, including excess stocks, spare productive capacity, demand cutbacks and international co-operation. The International Energy Agency has been criticised for not providing a co-ordinated programme for managing energy emergencies effectively[7]. This is a reason for reforming not abandoning the institution. Short-term emergency measures together with diversified sources of imports have an advantage over military deterrence and energy self-sufficiency; they can help to promote continuity of energy supplies not only from abroad but also from indigenous sources.

An energy strategy best fitted to cope with UK involvement in conventional war may well favour indigenous supplies, though existence of a two-way trade in energy could still be important. If the nation's survival was at risk it is reasonable to suppose that industrial disputes would not seriously threaten domestic fuel sources. But in the event of war, domestic stocks, pipelines and other supply facilities would be prime targets for the enemy. Diversified domestic sources of supply and the ability to import energy from allies might then be vital. If significant supplies of indigenous energy were considered to be strategic-ally important in the long run as well as the short run, then there is a clear case against pursuing self-sufficiency. Instead, cutting back domestic production and importing more of the country's needs, could prolong the time when strategically vital, diversified UK energy sources remained available.

A mix between imports and indigenous energy supplies, adequate emergency provisions (including import and export facilities) to cope with short-term disruptions, and diversified sources of supply, both domestic and foreign, would appear conducive to both economic and political well-being. The pursuit of energy self-sufficiency therefore appears inappropriate to both strategic and civil energy policy. Whether the mix of imports and indigenous supplies would be different for strategic reasons from the mix necessary for civil (economic and social reasons) requires detailed analysis beyond the scope of this study. Energy conditions in time of war might be different from those in peacetime, since both supply and demand might change. Energy require-ments for military purposes might increase, but the government would be more able to cut back demand in non-essential areas, without meeting consumer resistance. The benefits of strategic energy planning must also be clearly counted in terms of human life as well as economic and social well-being.

However, defences cannot render the UK one hundred per cent safe. Hence what should be sought is a desirable balance between marginal economic and national defence trade-offs. If strategic considerations dictated a high energy self-sufficiency ratio, then it might well be that the UK would have to trade off security of supply in peacetime (together with higher energy costs) against strategic security of supply. There could also be an intergenerational problem in that strategic energy security in the near term might be at the expense of acute strategic and civil vulnerability at a later stage.

Perceived security of supply

While it seems to us that energy self-sufficiency would not best promote the UK's security of supply (whether strategic or civil), there may well be a different relationship between self-sufficiency and perceived (rather than actual) security. Some people may _feel_ more secure if the whole of UK energy consumption can be provided from indigenous supplies. Consumers buy 'psychic' well-being in many ways and there is no reason why society, if it so desired, should not invest in energy projects, or deplete finite indigenous resources, so as to provide perceived security of supply by prolonging energy self-sufficiency for as long as possible. But all such purchases have an opportunity cost. Perceived security from energy self-sufficiency could be bought at the expense of actual security, both during the prolonged period of self-sufficiency and later, when the desired security-enhancing judicious mix between imports and indigenous supplies might be made more difficult to achieve.

Conclusions

Neither a priori reasoning nor evidence from the British energy market supports the view that energy self-sufficiency will promote security of supply. On the contrary, energy supplies are less secure under such a policy because indigenous supply disruptions (actual or threatened) are likely to be more frequent and more damaging. The costs of emergency provision against indigenous supply loss are also likely to be increased if there are no imports. If Britain adopted a specific long-term commitment to energy self-sufficiency, it could neither insulate itself from the repercussions of a crisis arising elsewhere in the international energy market, nor would it be wise to evade the costs of international co-operation to counter threats to international supplies and to cope with an emergency should it arise. The only real benefits gained would be avoidance of the immediate, direct effects from a cut-off specifically affecting the UK's own imported supplies. The security costs of adopting a policy of self-sufficiency are real if difficult to quantify; the intended benefits are largely illusory.

We would, therefore, argue that pursuing self-sufficiency for the sake of enhancing security of supply is a futile policy. 'Over-investment' in resources in the ground, in repletion and in demand-side conservation to promote self-sufficiency is likely to <u>reduce</u> the security of energy supplies. It seems <u>to us</u> that security of energy supplies above all else requires diversification of sources. It is not minimisation of energy imports via a self-sufficiency policy which is needed but the maintenance of a judicious balance between imports and indigenous supplies, and there should be diverse sources both of imports and of home supplies.

To promote diversification, there may well be a case for some 'over-investment'. For example, holding back some indigenous supplies for the future (thus reducing the self-sufficiency ratio below one) and importing to cover a a proportion of energy consumption during the next few years could be security-enhancing in two ways. First, such a move would provide diversified sources of supply in the present and, second, it would extend the length of time during which imports would be balanced with indigenous supplies. The latter point is particularly relevant to fuels where British reserves will probably have a lifetime of only a few decades, such as oil and gas, where to deplete more slowly in the coming decades and import some supplies instead could improve security of supply in the next century. Limited repletion and demand-side conservation policies not specifically aimed at self-sufficiency might also be justifiable for security reasons. As the UK again becomes a net fuel importer, probably in the 1990s, repletion and conservation which yielded or saved marginal quantities of indigenous energy might provide some additional security by helping to maintain the 'judicious balance' between imports and home supplies at which we have suggested Britain should aim.

If UK energy (especially oil and gas) is exported, it seems reasonable that a security premium be attached, thereby raising the price, because Britain may be sacrificing security of supply in the future whilst the importers gain in the present. Similarly, the possibility that it could export, or increase exports of, energy in an international emergency would be a particularly useful international precaution and should be valued accordingly.

We would not, however, wish to under-estimtae the practical difficulties of deciding how far to take output deferral, repletion and demand-side conservation. Calculating the possible security benefit to the UK of having indigenous energy far into the future is a virtually impossible task. The security premium attaching to indigenous supplies would vary with their marginal contribution to domestic consumption (and would probably disappear at self-sufficiency). But the optimal balance between imports and domestic supplies would itself tend to vary over time, depending on the structure of the home and international oil markets and on the substitutability of one fuel for another. The costs of extra energy investment to promote security would also need to include not only the direct costs but the indirect costs to the nation resulting from the increased monopolisation and politicisation of the energy market.

Notes

1. A fuller discussion of the recent history of British coal is in Robinson and Marshall, *What Future for British Coal?* and *What Future for British Coal Policy?* op.cit.

2. *Ibid.*

3. See for example, 'CEGB switches to oil to beat coal shortage', *The Financial Times*, 2 May 1984

4. M.A. Adelman, 'Coping with Supply Insecurity', *The Energy Journal*, April 1982.

5. See Chap. 4 note 5.

6. For a general discussion see D. Yergin and M. Hillenbrand (eds.) *Global Insecurity*, Houghton Mufflin, Boston, 1982, especially the chapter by Ian Smart.

7. See Adelman, *op.cit.*

Chapter Six

SELF-SUFFICIENCY AND ENERGY PRICES

One possible advantage of a self-sufficiency policy is that it might result in lower energy prices. In this chapter we examine whether there are indeed likely to be price-decreasing effects associated with a self-sufficiency policy, both internationally and domestically, and then consider whether there might also be price-increasing influences.

Effects on international energy prices: the large country or group case

One way in which a country's move from being a net energy importer to being self-sufficient (or a prolongation of self-sufficiency for a country which has already reached that state) might reduce internationally-traded fuel prices is by affecting the demand for foreign supplies of energy. For instance, a self-sufficiency policy might shift the demand curve for oil imports to the left, thus reducing the demand for imported oil at any given price and bringing about some reduction in prices. It might also flatten the curve (that is, make import demand more sensitive to price changes): thus the ability of overseas oil-producing countries to exploit the market might be diminished, and there might be a similar effect on other overseas energy suppliers.

These arguments undoubtedly have some force when applied to countries (such as the USA) or groups of countries (such as the European Economic Community or the members of the International Energy Agency[1]) which have large shares of world trade in oil or other forms of energy. Whether a policy which went as far as self-sufficiency would bring net benefits in terms of prices is, however, less clear. If a strict energy self-sufficiency policy were in operation, in the long run little could be gained from any reduction in world fuel prices which ensued; plainly, a fall in world prices could bring little or nothing in the way of direct benefits to a country or group which had minimal energy trade with the rest of the world. There might well be some minor indirect gains, for instance from a stimulus to world economic activity if any substantial international energy trade remained. Against these, however, would have to be offset any domestic price increases resulting from the accretion of monopoly power to indigenous fuel producers, as discussed at the end of this chapter.

An alternative would be a temporary energy self-sufficiency policy deliberately aimed at breaking the monopoly power of foreign suppliers. The favoured target for such a policy in the near future would most likely be the oil producers, though it is possible that in the more distant future monopoly problems will arise in other parts of the world energy market[2]. The idea would be that a large country or group would aim at self-sufficiency only for as long as necessary to bring down world energy prices; thereafter trade would resume and the importers would reap the benefits of lower prices.

The complications of devising and implementing such a policy would, however, be enormous. There are long lead times both on the supply and demand sides of the energy market. New supply facilities take many years to plan and construct, and there are also considerable time lags in implementing demand-saving measures except to the extent that they are merely 'housekeeping' changes which require little or no investment. A particular problem is that private companies, which foresaw that they would face import competition and lower prices at just about the time they would normally expect their investment in new energy supply facilities to come to fruition, would have no incentive whatsoever to invest without government guarantees of protection for many years ahead. Even if there were no explicit guarantees of protection if world energy prices were to fall, in the event of such a drop in prices there would be extremely strong pressures on government to exclude imports competitive with the energy supply facilities constructed during the self-sufficiency period. The lobbying power of companies which had invested in accordance with the self-sufficiency policy would be very considerable. Thus, in practice, it is quite likely that a 'temporary policy' would effectively turn into long-term protection.

Even if governments were to allow imports, the price reductions might well not persist. For a time, indigenous suppliers, with capital-intensive plants and therefore a high ratio of unavoidable to avoidable costs, might well meet import competition by pricing just above short-run marginal cost, thus bringing about some price reductions for fuel consumers both from imported and indigenous supplies. However, at prices which did not cover full costs and required returns on capital, investment in new indigenous supply facilities would be unattractive amd would diminish. Eventually, therefore, indigenous energy supplies would contract and the monopoly power of foreign suppliers would probably be restored.

For such reasons, a policy of 'switching on' and 'switching off' self-sufficiency would almost certainly be unsuccessful in a market with such long lead times as energy. There is a high probability that the policy would become permanent; if it did not, the chances are that the foreign monopolisation problem would re-appear in the 'switch off' period.

We would not go so far as to argue that, in the large country or group case, there is nothing which can be done to offset the market power of foreign suppliers. By a deliberate policy of marginally increasing indigenous fuel production and marginally decreasing fuel consumption, it might be possible to lower world fuel prices (or to prevent increases which would otherwise have occurred) and to take advantage of these relatively lower prices. However, such a policy would be quite different from self-sufficiency as generally understood. An alternative or complementary measure could be an international energy stockpile which, if large enough and administered effectively , might disrupt an energy cartel and lower the international price closer to a competitive level. Again, this is a very different policy option from energy self-sufficiency.

Effects on international energy prices: the UK case

The UK on its own is not a major force in world energy trade and its case is different from the one examined above. In general, it seems unlikely that pursuit of a self-sufficiency policy by the UK would in itself have any significant effect on world energy prices. To consider the case in more detail, however, we discuss below possible effects for each of the major internationally-traded fuels.

A policy close to self-sufficiency has been pursued for British coal in recent years[3]. Governments have generally been reluctant to allow any substantial quantities of imports (see Chapter 2) and exports have usually been small. The highest recent level of imports was in 1980, when they rose to about 7½ million tonnes from 4½ million tonnes in 1979, but from early 1981 onwards they were restricted, primarily by government pressure exerted on the Central Electricity Generating Board, and fell back to around 4 million tonnes a year from 1981 to 1983. The Coal Board increased its exports in 1981 and 1982 by pricing below full cost[4] so that Britain became a small net exporter of coal - about 5 million tonnes in 1981 and 3½ million tonnes in 1982. By 1983, however, net exports were only about 2 million tonnes. The coal self-sufficiency policy has probably raised prices in the British market by almost eliminating competition from imported steam coal, but the impact on international prices, if any, must have been very minor in view of the small size of the British coal trade. Given that Britain is so close to self-sufficiency in coal already, a move to complete self-sufficiency (or a move away) would be very unlikely to have any noticeable effect on world coal prices.

Natural gas trading policy has been almost the exact opposite of coal trading policy: gas exports have been banned by the government but imports by British Gas Corporation from the Norwegian part of the Frigg field (equivalent to nearly 25 per cent of UK gas consumption in 1983) have been permitted. Not only have there been no gas exports, but companies with discoveries were, with limited exceptions, permitted only to sell their gas in Britain to BGC prior to 1982. Until recently, therefore, British Gas was de facto sole buyer of natural gas from the North Sea and it was thus placed in an extremely powerful bargaining situation vis-a-vis the gas producers. The Oil and Gas (Enterprise) Act of 1982 allowed direct sales by gas producers to larger consumers (see Chapter 2), but the continuing ban on exports, combined with BGC's ability to import gas, has inevitably depressed the prices the Corporation pays for gas from the British sector of the North Sea[5] and probably prices to the Corporation's consumers. Because of the British ban on exports, gas prices in the rest of Western Europe have probably been a little higher than if exports had been allowed. If Britain were now to move to self-sufficiency in gas, presumably no more gas import contracts would be signed (though it would be some years before presently-contracted supplies ceased), exports would remain banned, and gas prices in Britain would tend to increase. Alternatively, there would be a balanced two-way trade in gas. Other things being equal, in either case gas prices in the rest of Europe would most likely decline a little relative to British prices. But, of course, with no gas trade, Britain could obtain no direct benefit from any such reduction.

The case of British oil is a little more complicated. It is quite reasonable to argue that, though Britain will generally be a price-taker in the world oil market, special circumstances in recent years have given it an influence on world prices[6]. During the period when world oil consumption started to decline, that is, from 1979 onwards, British oil production was still rising substantially. Between 1978 and 1983 UK annual production more than doubled, from 54 to nearly 115 million tonnes. Output from other non-OPEC areas - such as Mexico and Alaska - was also rising and the effect was almost certainly to depress world oil prices.

However, the rapid rise in UK production seems to have been a consequence of structural changes in the world oil industry - which made non-OPEC sources relatively attractive to the international oil companies as compared with OPEC oil[7] - rather than the result of a deliberate self-sufficiency policy by the British government. As we have seen (Chapter 2), governments were for many years happy enough with a 'rapid development' oil and gas policy, and so far they have evidently taken no positive steps to encourage self-sufficiency per se. Had they wished to do so, they would have cut back oil production from 1980 onwards to the level of home consumption, by direct limitations of production or exports.

Whatever effect British oil production has so far had on world prices, its impact in future seems likely to be small. As explained in Chapter 3, production is now well in excess of UK oil consumption and is close to its peak. A self-sufficiency policy for oil would therefore involve cutting back net exports to around zero during the 1980s, the early 1990s and possibly beyond[8]. To reduce production into equality with indigenous consumption might mean lowering net annual crude oil exports by 10-15 million tonnes or so on average in the rest of the 1980s (though there would probably be bigger cutbacks in the mid-1980s), and there might also be some reductions in the 1990s. Given that annual world crude oil exports are over 1000 million tonnes, the effect on world prices would probably be very small. However, since the UK would be starting from a net export position, any impact there might be would be slightly price-increasing during the period when the country would otherwise have been a net exporter. Thereafter, there could be some slight price-decreasing effect because Britain would be self-sufficient instead of becoming a net oil importer.

In general, it seems to us unlikely that a self-sufficiency policy for a country of the UK's size in world energy trade would have any substantial effect on world energy prices. Moreover, whatever minor effects there might be, there remains the same paradox as for a larger country or group: even if world fuel prices could be depressed by a self-sufficiency policy, there is no way a country or group which had effectively excluded itself from the world market could take direct advantage of the lower prices.

Lower prices for indigenous supplies?

If there is no significant direct advantage from lower world prices which Britain can capture by pursuing a self-sufficiency policy, any price gains would have to accrue via lower-priced indigenous supplies. That is, the self-sufficiency policy would by some means have to bring the price of home-produced energy below what it would have been under conditions in which fuels were more freely traded.

According to our estimates (Chapter 3), with unchanged government policy Britain would most likely remain a net energy exporter during the 1980s and possibly in the early 1990s as well. From around 1990, however, the chances are that the UK would once more become a net importer of energy. If government policy was to maintain a self-sufficiency ratio of about one from now onwards (either by eliminating trade or by maintaining a balance between imports and exports), the effect would therefore be:

- in the next ten years or so, to eliminate net exports which would otherwise have occurred.
- in subsequent years, to eliminate the net imports there would otherwise have been.

As a first approximation, one might expect the effect of a self-sufficiency policy to be supply-increasing, price-decreasing in the first period and supply-decreasing, price-increasing in the second period. But we need to look more closely at the influence of such a policy on costs and price-setting before we draw any firm conclusions.

The 1980s and early 1990s

During the first period, when Britain would otherwise have been a net exporter, a self-sufficiency policy would have to find a means of reducing exports or increasing imports. Chapter 4 explains the alternative possibilities and suggests that the most likely means of implementing a self-sufficiency policy in this period would be by reducing crude oil production and therefore exports. We also explain there some of the complications of such a policy.

As regards prices, there could be some temporary decreasing impact during the period when net exports were being reduced, since some of the oil not exported might find its way to the British market, thereby increasing supplies. The rate of production which would equate with home consumption would be difficult to estimate in advance, and it would probably become a subject of negotiation between oil companies and government. The companies would have an incentive to keep up their production because of low avoidable costs relative to prices and heavy unavoidable (sunk) costs. Thus it is possible that supplies to the British market would for a time be somewhat higher, so that oil prices (and possibly the prices of competitive fuels) would be rather lower under this kind of self-sufficiency policy than on our policy unchanged assumption.

But there would be other results of production or export control which could tend to raise prices. As explained in our oil self-sufficiency study, any form of depletion control would reduce the attractiveness of investment in the British North Sea unless the government offered compensating inducements to the oil companies. Thus, without such inducements, investment in oil exploration and production would be depressed so that by the 1990s crude oil output would most likely be below the figures suggested in Chapter 3 which assumed no depletion controls. Moreover, political regulation of production might initially increase uncertainty (especially if the major political parties differed on the extent and mechanisms of control), which again would tend to decrease investment and the availability of technical expertise from abroad. Consequently, with a self-sufficiency policy in operation, governments would almost certainly be driven into offering various inducements to the oil companies to restore their profitability and to stimulate production. One means of raising profits would be to increase crude oil prices above the world level, which would raise oil product prices to consumers unless the government provided subsidies (in which case taxpayers would bear the cost of the policy).

It is now time to look at the longer run during which, in the absence of policy change, the UK would revert to being a net importer of energy. This period is likely to begin around the year 1990, so if governments wished to preserve self-sufficiency they would, given the long lead times in the energy market, need to take action in the very near future. We consider what arguments might be used to suggest that in the longer run self-sufficiency would bring cost and price advantages.

Reducing costs in the long run

One case which could be put by self-sufficiency advocates is that Britain's fuel industries need a temporary period of protection during which, by excluding cheaper imports, energy prices would be higher than they would otherwise have been. The period of protection would allow the industries to realise economies of scale, invest to take advantage of the latest technology, and generally lower their costs. At the end of this period, it may be argued, protection will be unnecessary since Britain's energy costs and prices will be competitive with those of other countries. The case is similar to one which is sometimes made for temporarily sheltering 'infant industries', especially in developing countries, until they are sufficiently mature and reach the minimum efficient scale which allows them to stand up to overseas competition.

Whatever the strength of the case in the developing world, we doubt whether Britain has any true 'infants' in its major fuel industries. The organisations which run these industries are large, sophisticated bodies. It would be surprising indeed if they needed to grow any larger to reap unrealised technical economies of scale at plant level or managerial economies at firm level.

That does not, of course, mean that these organisations will not occasionally use infant-industry-type arguments. But such arguments should be seen as part of the lobbying and bargaining process between large corporations (especially those which are nationalised) and the government which we discuss later in this chapter. The coal industry, for example, has on numerous occasions contended that it needs a breathing space of several years in which to invest so that it can become competitive[9]: during the breathing space there would be a minimum output commitment from the government and/or import controls. So far, however, though several breathing spaces have been allowed by governments of different parties, Britain has not yet seen the emergence of a low-cost coal industry because of the failure to close high-cost capacity on a sufficient scale.

The major problem we see in infant-industry or breathing-space type arguments is that, during the period of protection, the incentive to become efficient is almost inevitably lessened as compared with a more competitive situation. The organisations which are sheltered are, in effect, granted more monopoly power by the government giving them the potential to increase prices. This encourages 'organisational slack'[10], costs increase and prices therefore rise. The ability of the organisations to extract favours from government by lobbying is also increased. Even if protection is said to be time-limited, big corporations employing large numbers have considerable leverage, and it is never difficult for those directly affected to find some compelling reason why protection should be extended a little longer. It is also quite possible, as theorists in the economics of bureaucracy have argued, that government bureaucrats will identify with the industry view and provide support for it. The voice of the consumer, however, is little heard and little heeded, because the costs of abandoning protection are concentrated and seem obvious, whereas the benefits are thinly spread and have no substantial effect on any one pressure group. Consequently, 'temporary' periods of protection all too easily result in long-run costs and prices which are higher than they would otherwise have been.

A recent example of the way in which time limits can readily be breached occurred in 1981. An apparently very determined attempt by the Conservative government elected in 1979 to place a time limit on subsidies for the National Coal Board resulted in the 1980 Coal Industry Act (see Chapters 2 and 5). By the early months of 1981, however, the government was forced, under threat of strikes, both to extend the time limit and to increase the subsidies. Then, in 1983, another Coal Industry Bill was introduced which again provided for increased subsidies and put off the time when they would be eliminated.

A rather similar argument for government aid to established indigenous fuel industries is that new energy sources which might be important in the long run will only appear if public money is spent on them. There is, for instance, a case for government support for basic research in the energy industries along the lines that such research is a 'public good'[11], the results of which will be disseminated throughout society and cannot be appropriated by those who pursue the research. Support can also be justified for

energy sources which seem likely to be
environmentally more benign than those we now use,
since they will avoid some of the pollution costs
which society would otherwise incur. In addition,
there may be an argument (similar to that for
infant industries) for public support for research
and development in the energy industries which
seems likely to pay off only in the very long run
(if at all). Research into some renewable forms
of energy and into nuclear fusion fall into this
category. There is, however, a danger that such
long-term R and D support, once started, can be
very difficult ever to reduce. Particularly in
high technology fields, organisations may appear
which become champions of 'big-science' projects
and which can become very powerful advocates
vis-a-vis politicians and civil servants who are
relatively lacking in expertise. The high
proportion of spending on long-run nuclear
technologies in total public sector energy R and
D, and the long-standing nature of this spending,
may be examples of this phenomenon.

Government assistance to promote long-run
energy sources is unlikely to help significantly
in promoting self-sufficiency in the period with
which we are concerned. Even if it could, there
is no reason to believe that, in supporting any
'infants' and aiding the development of energy
resources for the long term, governments should
aim at equating home production with home
consumption. They should, more properly, compare
the expected marginal costs of such support with
expected marginal benefits. They might well then
conclude that a certain amount of assistance can
reasonably be advocated on 'judicious mix'
grounds, since, in addition to possible
environmental benefits, production of some new
forms of energy for the long term-future should
help to promote security of supply and may keep
down fuel prices.

Avoiding unexpectedly high long-run world energy prices

As well as the belief that self-sufficiency can
provide lower long-run energy costs by promoting
economies of scale and protecting infant
industries, an argument implicit in the views of
self-sufficiency advocates is that it would
protect against unexpectedly high world energy
prices, arising either because of increasing

scarcity or because of resource monopolisation. The case seems to be that the UK should preserve its own fuel industries (even when they appear relatively high-cost) and prepare well in advance for the time when world prices may rise because of the lead times in building new supply facilities. In effect, that is one of the reasons for protection given in the 1965 Fuel Policy White Paper (see Chapter 2), which faded into the background until it was resurrected by the oil shocks of the 1970s.

Concern about the effects of unexpectedly high future energy prices generally stems from the belief that natural resource markets are myopic and tend to under-predict prices. If that were so, 'too much' energy would be produced in the near term and 'too little' held back for the long-run future. These tendencies would be reinforced if private sector discount rates exceeded social discount rates. Thus, the contention is that governments should intervene to ensure that depletion rates of non-renewable energy resources (and investment in renewable resources and demand-side conservation) reflect higher price expectations and lower discount rates. More indigenous energy would then be produced in the long-run future and there would be some protection against future prices higher than predicted by the market. There is, of course, nothing in such arguments to suggest that self-sufficiency should be the policy objective, and, in any case, they are over-simplified.

First, the reason why markets fail to foresee long-run energy price movements is because of the inherent difficulty of exercising such foresight. There is no reason to believe politicians and bureaucrats will be more successful; on the contrary, market participants have a bigger incentive to predict with reasonable accuracy since they are staking their shareholders' money when they act on their expectations.

Second, markets will not necessarily under-predict prices. Governments which intervene on the assumption that they are so doing - and, for example, defer production of fossil fuel resources - are liable to make major errors of direction. To illustrate, a government which insisted on holding large quantities of oil in the ground in the belief that there would be an upsurge in real crude oil prices in the long run

would encumber society with heavy opportunity cuts
if the real price were actually to fall.

An insurance premium for indigenous supplies?

A similar argument to the contention that markets
are myopic is that, though future movements are to
all intents and purposes unforeseeable, an
insurance premium should be attached to the value
of future indigenous energy production to guard
against the possibility that, in the long run,
imported energy prices might go very high and
cause extensive economic and social damage. There
is some substance in this argument, if there is
genuine reason to believe that society is willing
to incur the cost, but it clearly does not lead to
the conclusion that self-sufficiency should be the
aim. The insurance premium should be assessed by
evaluating the probability of occurrence of very
high prices, then calculating the associated costs
to society and determining society's attitude to
risk. After all these extremely difficult
calculations had been performed, it would be
surprising indeed if the conclusion was that the
optimal solution was for home consumption and home
production to be equated. On the whole, it seems
to us more probable that, if insurance is
highly valued, production should be cut below the
self-sufficiency level so that substantial
quantities of output are 'banked' for the more
distant future when imports would otherwise
account for a large part of energy supplies.

Monopolies, lobbies and fuel prices

In this chapter, as in Chapter 5, we have
emphasised the monopoly problems to which a policy
of self-sufficiency tends to lead. We now draw
attention more explicitly to how monopolisation
might be expected to influence fuel prices.

Following a temporary period of fuel 'surplus'
in the next ten years or so, during which a
self-sufficiency policy would have to reduce net
exports of fuel, such a policy would in the longer
term have to aim at avoiding the net fuel imports
which would be likely if policy remained
unchanged. To some extent, more forceful
'conservation' measures could help by reducing the
demand from fuel consumers (see Chapter 4), but

the deliberate promotion of self-sufficiency would almost certainly have to include measures (such as subsidies, taxes or direct controls) which would increase home supplies at the expense of foreign supplies. Thus competition from imports would be restricted and prices would tend to increase.

In theory, various price-decreasing influences could then begin to work, though, as explained earlier in this chapter, we are doubtful whether they would do so. World energy prices might be somewhat reduced, though that would be a most unlikely consequence of the pursuit of self-sufficiency in Britain alone, and in any case the country could benefit very little from them if it remained self-sufficient. The prices of indigenous supplies might be reduced by a temporary phase of protection which allowed home energy suppliers to reduce their costs and new energy forms to appear, though in practice the incentive to reduce costs would be slight under protection and what was initially intended to be temporary might well become permanent. There might be some hope of avoiding unexpected fuel price increases originating abroad, though we have expressed doubts as to whether self-sufficiency would have that effect.

These arguments and counter-arguments seem to us to leave considerable doubts as to whether lower long-run prices would result from a policy of energy self-sufficiency. Consequently, from what we have already said, it seems that we might effectively raise our energy costs in the medium term only to receive future 'benefits' which could be negative and, at best, seem likely to be very small. The real underlying problem with a declared policy of self-sufficiency is that, whatever the initial state of the fuel market, a reduction of trade with the outside world would inevitably increase the market power of home suppliers. By 'market power' in this context we mean more than monopoly power in the sense of the output-restricting, price-increasing firm of elementary economic theory. We mean also the increased lobbying power of large organisations which would result from the increased politicisation of energy market decision-making under a regime of greater government control.

If the problem was simply one of private monopoly, one could be relatively unconcerned since private monopolies tend, in the long run, to be undermined by the normal forces of the market. Private companies cannot, in practice, exclude all competition for long. If they exploit their market power, their field of activity will appear relatively profitable and other organisations will find means of moving into it, thus tending to compete away 'excess' profits. Often the competition will come from large companies, well-established in other markets, which are always seeking profitable diversification opportunities.

However, we are, by definition, not considering a case in which normal market forces are allowed to operate. A deliberate policy of achieving or (in Britain's case) maintaining self-sufficiency means that the government in one way or another shelters indigenous fuel producers from overseas competition. Since these constraints on competition must persist so long as the self-sufficiency policy is in operation, the ability of market forces to restrain the exercise of producer power is inevitably limited in the long run as well as the short run. Of course, it is possible for the government itself to regulate the monopolies it creates. But it is very difficult to obtain the results of competition in the absence of competitive forces.

Competition in the British energy market is already limited by government action; three of the fuel supply industries are run by public corporations, and there are various taxes, subsidies and direct controls (see Chapter 2) which restrict competition. Once government enters into such activities, it becomes advantageous for the fuel suppliers to spend time and money on lobbying because the potential gains are very considerable. The scope for gains would only be increased if the government declared its aim to be self-sufficiency, because large organisations would attempt to trade their ability to provide more energy against the aid they would claim to be necessary. Making such trades might become even more important than competing in the economic market place.

If the long-term aim of government was to limit the British energy market to British suppliers, competitive pressures would be significantly eased and collusion would become simpler. It would be even more difficult than it is now for government to judge the investment proposals of the nationalised industries, since there would be no direct standard of foreign

competition against which to judge them.
Government would also have to make judgements
about the investment proposals of private fuel
suppliers to the extent that they were put forward
as means of enhancing self-sufficiency. The
result of attempts to control nationalised
industries in Britain is hardly encouraging. The
industries, which do not have clear guidelines,
very naturally form and pursue corporate
objectives, rather than the 'national interest'
aims once anticipated by idealists. Government
becomes concerned about these centres of corporate
power and therefore continually interferes,
causing confusion in managerial objectives and
promoting inefficiency. It also regularly yields
to the temptation to use the industries as
macro-economic regulators: for instance, it may
hold down their prices to reduce measured
inflation or it may raise their prices to reduce
public borrowing. Under a régime of
self-sufficiency, it seems likely that these kinds
of problems would be multiplied, and that there
would be a state of continuous bargaining between
fuel producers and government with no effective
means of protecting the interests of consumers.

Conclusions

It appears to us that the outcome of a
self-sufficiency policy should not be judged
merely in terms of the kind of economic theory
which is based on standard welfare economics with
intervention practised by an omniscient,
altruistic government. In these terms, it is just
possible (though unlikely, given our limited
low-cost resource base) that lower long-run prices
could be the result of pursuing self-sufficiency
rather than allowing imports, because government
would effectively control incipient monopolistic
tendencies in the indigenous industries.
Real-world governments, however, are composed of
people joining together in shifting coalitions and
bargaining with (and frequently identifying with)
well-informed organised producers. In such a
system, to declare a policy of self-sufficiency
seems almost certain to increase the power of
producers, both in the economic and in the
political market-places. It is very difficult to
believe that, in such circumstances, lower prices
would be the outcome: the recent history of coal,

where a policy similar to self-sufficiency has been in operation, seems to suggest strongly that the interests of consumers will be disregarded and that higher not lower prices will result.

In Chapter 5 we argued that a judicious mix of indigenous supplies and imports is needed to promote security of supply. We would also contend that a similar mix, rather than self-sufficiency, is required to obtain the beneficial effects of competitive pressures on the long-run movement of indigenous energy prices and to protect against unforeseeably high world energy prices in the very long term.

Notes

1. The idea that policies which reduce oil consumption are desirable is implicit in many of the publications of the International Energy Agency. See, for example, IEA, Energy Policies and Programmes of IEA Countries: 1982 Review, OECD, Paris, 1983.

2. There could, for example, be monopolistic tendencies in international gas markets. World coal markets seem less open to monopolisation because of the widespread nature of reserves, the lack of concentration of ownership and the absence of serious barriers to entry. See OECD, Steam Coal - Prospects to 2000, HMSO, 1978.

3. See Robinson and Marshall, What Future for British Coal?, and What Future for British Coal Policy?, op.cit.

4. See Pit Closures, Second Report from the House of Commons Select Committee on Energy, Session 1982-83, December 1982.

5. Robinson, 'The Errors of North Sea Policy', op.cit.

6. Robinson and Morgan, op.cit. chap. 1.

7. J.E. Hartshorn, 'Re-cast rôles in the world oil performance', Middle East Economic Survey, 24 October 1983.

8. A more detailed discussion of an oil self-sufficiency is in Robinson and Marshall, Oil's Contribution to UK Self-sufficiency?, op.cit.

9. Robinson and Marshall, What Future for British Coal?, op.cit.

10. The concept of 'organisational slack' is discussed in R.M. Cyert and J.G. March, A Behavioral Theory of the Firm, Prentice Hall, New York, 1963.

11. See note 5, Chap. 4.

Chapter Seven

SOME MACRO-ECONOMIC EFFECTS OF A SELF-SUFFICIENCY POLICY

A policy of self-sufficiency in a sector of the
economy as large as energy would inevitably have
significant direct and indirect macro-economic
consequences. Because many forms of energy are
traded internationally, the most obvious impact
would be on the balance of payments, but there
could also be effects on employment, the rate of
economic growth, the rate of price inflation,
government tax revenues and the distribution of
income. The purpose of this chapter is to discuss
briefly what some of these effects might be, using
the same time horizon (2020) as in earlier
chapters and continuing to distinguish between two
periods.

In the first of these, which we refer to as
the 'deferral period', some UK energy production
would initially be held back, avoiding the net
energy exports which would otherwise have
occurred: in practice, as explained in Chapter 4,
it is oil output which would most likely be
deferred, so we are essentially considering a
policy of <u>oil</u> production deferral in this
period[1]. Then, in the latter part of the deferral
period, the reserves previously held off the
market would be produced in order to maintain
self-sufficiency.

The second period (the 'repletion period') is
one in which UK self-sufficiency could no longer
be extended by output deferral. As a temporary
expedient, there might be a policy of <u>accelerated</u>
depletion so as to maintain self-sufficiency for a
few years. However, the main policy character-
istic of this period would be an attempt to
increase indigenous energy production by the
various means described in Chapter 4, such as more

liberal licensing, subsidies, tax concesssions and price increases. In both the deferral and the repletion periods there might also be demand-side action to reduce energy consumption per unit of output by means of taxes, subsidies or direct controls.

The deferral period

During the relatively short deferral period (see Chapters 3 and 4), both indigenous energy production and net exports of energy would initially be reduced and then later would be increased, compared with a situation in which there was no self-sufficiency policy. The distinguishing feature of the early depletion period would be 'over-investment' in resources in the ground (Chapter 4), which is a form of investment with no associated output or employment. Consequently, the early direct effects of the deferral policy (other things being equal) would be tendencies for real gross domestic product and employment to be reduced and for the current account balance of payments to deteriorate. Later in the deferral period there would be contrary tendencies as deferred output was brought back.

Over the period as a whole, since the quantity of energy produced would be approximately the same as if there had been no output deferral policy, there should be no significant differences in real GDP, employment and the current account balance of payments. Nevertheless, the losses would occur early in the deferral period and the gains later. Therefore, assuming a positive social discount rate and abstracting from possible social benefits of the kind discussed in Chapters 5 and 6, there would be some social welfare loss in present value terms. As we have explained, production of oil is more likely to be deferred than production of other forms of energy. Consequently, our conclusion is consistent with one we have stated elsewhere[2] with respect to oil output deferral - that, any social benefits aside, such a policy would probably significantly reduce the present value of the UK's oil reserves.

The above description is, however, a simplified and mechanistic account of direct effects on production, employment and overseas payments. In practice, various adjustment processes would act (though imperfectly and with significant time lags) to modify incipient effects on real GDP, employment and overseas payments. For example, energy prices may tend to be reduced in the early deferral period and increased later, as explained in Chapter 6. Thus there might be some early gains in terms of a slightly lower general price level, offset by a higher general price level later.

Exchange-rate variations would also have some compensating effects. Since net energy exports would be reduced in the early deferral period and increased later (as compared with a situation in which there was no self-sufficiency policy), the exchange rate may at first be lower and then later be higher than without a self-sufficiency policy. As a result, (unless exchange-rate effects were completely offset by faster inflation, for instance because of increased domestic factor payments) British goods would become more competitive relative to foreign goods both at home and abroad, so stimulating UK output and employment and improving the current balance of payments in the early deferral period. In the later deferral period there would be contrary effects. Consequently, over the deferral period as a whole, exchange-rate movements might be expected to even out changes in employment, real GDP and the current balance of payments, even though the smoothing process would be impeded by factor immobility and other market imperfections. Variations in wages and other factor payments might have similar smoothing effects: for instance, the tendency for employment to be reduced in the early deferral period might be partially counteracted by lower wages than there would be in the absence of an output deferral policy.

Another effect, which would reinforce the depressing impact on production and employment of the early stages of a deferral policy, would occur because of the changed time distribution of government tax revenues during the deferral period. Delaying oil production in the early deferral period would mean delaying the receipt of substantial oil tax revenues: in 1983/4 offshore oil and gas yielded about £9 billion[3] in taxes or approximately 8 per cent of total central government receipts. Thus in the early deferral period, as oil tax revenues fell (compared with a 'policy unchanged' situation), governments would either have to trim spending or increase non-oil taxation or permit a rise in public borrowing which would tend to raise interest rates.

Overall, our view of the macro-economic effects of a production deferral policy designed to maintain self-sufficiency is as follows. If one assumes that the very considerable practical difficulties of successfully implementing a deferral policy can be overcome, that the adjustment processes we have described operate (albeit imperfectly), and that productive factors are reasonably mobile, then the impact on the economy should be quite limited. Nevertheless, such impact as occurred would probably be adverse. Cutting back oil exports to prolong self-sufficiency would lead, directly and indirectly, to some reduction in production and employment in oil and associated industries which would not be made up for a number of years. If deferral were combined with demand-side action to reduce energy consumption per unit of output, there might be some increase in employment in relatively labour-intensive 'conservation' activities. However, if governments were pursuing strict self-sufficiency, the levels of energy output at which they would aim would be lower with a conservation policy in operation than without such a policy: consequently, employment in oil, other energy and related industries would be correspondingly lower.

One claim which is sometimes made is that some of the adjustment processes we have described could be so managed by government as to allow Britain to make a smoother transition from net exporter to net importer of oil. It has, for example, been suggested that levelling out the 'hump' of British oil production would avoid an excessive appreciation of sterling followed by a subsequent sharp decline; thus structural changes in the British economy associated with oil would be less violent[4] and Britain's eventual re-entry into the world oil market would be eased. It is now too late to arrange a gradual build-up of North Sea production, with the aim of minimising structural change in the economy. It would, however, be possible for a far-sighted and benevolent government, starting from the peak of oil production in the mid-1980s, to cut oil production for several years, 'filling in' later with deferral output and thereby arranging a

smoother and more gradual production decline than
would otherwise occur. Structural changes away
from oil would thus occur at a less damaging rate
than if production were not planned in this way.

In practice, regulating production so as to
achieve such a smooth transition would be
extremely difficult. Moreover, we have doubts
whether politicians would act in this far-sighted
manner, given that they would, in effect, be
deferring macro-economic benefits they could have
obtained, bequeathing them instead to future
administrations. If, however, we make the heroic
assumptions that the practical problems of
regulation could be overcome and that politicians
would be willing to defer macro-economic gains,
there seems to be no case to support deferral to
prolong self-sufficiency. In principle, one might
advocate cutting oil production to less than that
needed to maintain self-sufficiency, so as to
achieve a long period of slowly declining output
which resulted in a gradual increase in import
dependence and relatively slow structural change
in the economy (assisted by a progressive
depreciation of sterling). But maintaining self-
sufficiency by a deferral regime would be a
strictly time-limited policy: at some stage,
filling in with deferred output would cease to
sustain self-sufficiency and a step-change to
substantial import dependence would ensue unless
the government had embarked on a repletion policy
(see next section). The economy would then have
to cope with a more difficult transition than if
the government had not intervened at all, but had
allowed the exchange rate to perform its slow and
imperfect smoothing function during an oil output
decline which promises to be fairly gradual
anyway (without any more government action).

Similar arguments apply to another popular
belief - that by production deferral the rate of
decline of the now considerable government
revenues from offshore oil and gas production
could be made more gradual. In that way, the
budgetary and macro-economic management problems
of falling oil revenues would apparently be made
less severe. It is true that the decline in oil
tax revenues could be smoothed by a careful
deferral policy. However, it is also true that
the appropriate policy would not be one of
maintaining self-sufficiency for as long as
possible. Just as such a policy would eventually
bring a step-change to much greater import

dependence, it would at the same time bring a sharp drop in oil revenues (in the absence of repletion). Budgetary and economic management problems would at that time become more severe, not easier.

As explained above, the decline in oil output (and, most likely, in oil tax revenues also) may well be fairly gradual without any government action. A far-sighted government which was, nevertheless, concerned about the impact of the decline might indulge in some judicious deferral. It might also take other policy steps, such as gradually introducing an import tariff on crude oil[5] (so as to replace some of the 'lost' revenues from indigenous production and, at the same time, promote energy conservation), if it could do so without retaliation by other countries against British exports. Alternatively, and for similar reasons, taxes on petroleum products consumed in the UK could be increased. Whatever the policies adopted, it is difficult to think of circumstances in which deferral to prolong self-sufficiency would be appropriate.

The repletion period

There are bound to be considerable time lags between the implementation of government 'repletion' measures, such as tax concessions or subsidies, and any resulting increase in indigenous energy output. Consequently, long before the deferral period was over, a government intent on prolonging self-sufficiency well into next century would have to introduce such measures. The question to be considered here is the extent to which 'over-investment' in repletion (see Chapter 4) would yield macro-economic benefits. Possible gains in terms of security of supply and energy prices are discussed in Chapters 5 and 6.

Unlike the deferral period, in the repletion period there would be no obvious initial costs in terms of lower GDP, exports and employment which would have to be offset against corresponding improvements later. There would, however, be opportunity costs in employing resources in repletion rather than elsewhere, unless those resources would otherwise have been idle (see below). Another difference, as compared with the deferral period, is that energy production resulting from repletion measures would, without those measures, have been judged unprofitable by private and public energy corporations; otherwise the production would have taken place without need for government stimulus.

Both deferral and repletion imply 'over-investment', as explained in Chapter 4. But, to take the example of oil, a barrel of oil deferred is different from a barrel of 'repleted oil'. Deferral means that a barrel which would have been produced at one time is delayed until later and thereby rendered less profitable in present value terms to the company concerned (unless prices net of costs and taxes rise at a percentage rate in excess of the discount rate). Repletion, except when it is merely the temporary expedient of accelerated depletion, means that barrels which would not have been produced at all without a policy change come on to the market.

In effect energy repletion, whether or not it goes as far as self-sufficiency, involves giving up some trade in energy which would otherwise have taken place, thereby relinquishing the gains which producers and consumers perceived to be associated with that trade. Assuming that demand is unaffected, a corresponding quantity of indigenous energy, which would have been unable to compete against imports without government assistance, is produced instead. The initial impact of higher indigenous energy output might bring some increase in real GDP and employment and an improved balance of payments, leading subsequently to similar secondary effects to those described earlier (for instance, an appreciation of sterling which might offset some of the initial gains).

Whatever the immediate impact and the apparent macro-economic advantages of repletion - indicated, for example, by an improved balance of trade in energy - the danger is that this kind of policy would merely bring early cosmetic benefits which concealed real longer-term losses as the gains from trade were sacrificed and resources were less efficiently used. The distribution of resources in the British economy is no doubt far from the hypothetical 'optimum' and the trade which takes place with other countries is nowhere near the theoretical ideal. Nevertheless, the substitution of indigenous for imported energy as a result of government aid could well make the distribution of resources worse, leading to excessive investment in home-produced energy and higher energy costs (as compared with the alternative of importing) which would feed through into the costs of goods produced in Britain. In such circumstances, the rate of economic growth would probably be reduced, and the chances are that employment would be lower, the current balance of payments would be worse, and the general price level would be higher (although sudden, sharp price increases resulting from energy 'shocks' abroad might be avoided, as explained in Chapter 6).

These consequences are not inevitable. Although 'repleted energy' would be produced only because of government assistance, it is conceivable that repletion measures would result in the exploitation of scale economies which would not otherwise have been realised, in technological advances or in the unexpected discovery of low-cost energy sources. It is also possible that a repletion programme combined with measures to promote energy conservation could lead to offsetting employment creation in labour-intensive conservation activities (such as home insulation). But real-world repletion programmes would also be likely to bring monopolisation, lobbying and a general politicisation of the energy market for the reasons given in Chapters 5 and 6. We are therefore doubtful whether any real long-term macro-economic benefits would accrue from a repletion policy, though it might well be possible to point to some statistics, such as the energy balance of trade and employment in the energy industries, which indicated apparent gains.

In principle, to evaluate whether and to what extent there should be repletion to capture macro-economic benefits one should analyse the marginal social costs and marginal social benefits of alternative repletion measures. To trace the impact of these measures on the economy and to quantify all the related social costs and benefits is, unfortunately, a task beyond present methods of economic analysis and economic modelling. However, there are some statements one can make about the likely results of such an evaluation. For example, it would be a remarkable coincidence if repletion to the extent of self-sufficiency was shown to be the optimum policy for realising macro-economic benefits. As we have pointed out

in earlier chapters, there is no reason whatsoever
to believe that equating indigenous energy
production with home consumption is the most
appropriate goal of repletion policy. Indeed,
there are clear indications to the contrary. A
self-sufficientenergy market would give rise to
greater problems of politicisation and
monopolisation (and hence higher costs and prices)
than if lower degrees of repletion were the
objective. Moreover, self-sufficiency maintained
through repletion would aggravate re-entry into
the world energy market in the same way as would
self-sufficiency via production deferral: at the
end of the period during which self-sufficiency
could be sustained there would be a step-change in
output and severe structural adjustment problems
in the economy.

Therefore, in our view, there is a clear
presumption against repletion to attain
self-sufficiency as a means of obtaining macro-
economic benefits, just as there are similar
presumptions on security and price grounds.
Nevertheless, there may well be some degree of
repletion which, if we could identify and attain
it, would bring macro-economic advantages. If,
for example, the resources employed as part of a
repletion programme would otherwise have been
unused (so that their opportunity cost is
apparently zero), there may be gains to be
realised from employing them. That is an argument
sometimes used for keeping open 'uneconomic'
British coal mines. However, even in such cases
the advantages are not as clear as they might
seem. There are many socially desirable projects
other than energy repletion which could be
undertaken; therefore there might be an
opportunity cost in using for repletion even
those resources which were unemployed at the time
repletion began. We also have some reservations
about recommending limited repletion because we
suspect it would be very difficult to keep a
repletion programme within tight limits. The
programmes would inevitably stimulate industry
lobbying which would be hard for governments to
resist, and the eventual result might be to give
the industry concerned considerable leverage over
the rest of the community. As explained in
Chapters 5 and 6, that seems to us to have been
the consequence of government efforts to keep up
coal production in Britain by subsidies and import
restrictions.

Macro-economic effects

Other economic and social consequences also need consideration by a government contemplating energy repletion for macro-economic reasons. In particular, we would point to some possible distributional effects. By and large, we would expect that the greater the degree of repletion the greater would be the bargaining strength of indigenous energy producers and the more would be the re-distribution of income away from consumers and towards those producers. Since energy is a commodity with a low income elasticity of demand - so that poorer consumers spend on fuel and light relatively high proportions of their income - this kind of re-distribution would be regressive (unless compensated) and it is difficult to believe that society would knowingly undertake it.

We would conclude that, just as there is a case in principle for a degree of energy production deferral to realise macro-economic benefits, there is also some case for energy repletion, though we have doubts whether, in practice, it would bring macro-economic gains. Whether or not our scepticism about the benefits of repletion are justified, one thing seems clear: self-sufficiency is not an appropriate aim of repletion policy any more than it is of a deferral programme.

Notes

1.   See   Robinson   and   Marshall,   Oil's Contribution   to   UK   Self-Sufficiency,   op.cit., (especially Chaps. 4 and 5), which explores in more detail the economic and political issues raised by an oil production deferral programme.

2.   Ibid., Chap. 4.

3.   Department of Energy, Development of the Oil and Gas Resources of the United Kingdom, 1984, HMSO, London, April 1984.

4.   For   instance,   T.   Barker,   'Depletion policy   and   de-industrialisation   of   the   UK economy', Energy Economics, April 1981.

5.   Oil import tariffs have been recommended by several economists in the United States.   See, for example, William W. Hogan, 'Energy Policy and the Reagan Experiment', 1981-82, Discussion Paper E-84-01, Energy and Environmental Policy Center, John F. Kennedy School of Government, Harvard University, February 1984, pp. 20-3.

Chapter Eight

DISTANT GENERATIONS

A self-sufficiency policy of the kind discussed in earlier chapters would defer oil production for a period and take longer-term measures such as cutting energy demand, increasing output of indigenous fossil fuels and renewables, and expanding the nuclear power programme. However, there are alternative forms of self-sufficiency policy. For instance, 'environmentalists' and 'conservationists' frequently advocate a future characterised by low energy consumption supplied by indigenous renewable energy sources. In the transition to this 'low energy future' there would be a rapid and wide-ranging programme to cut energy demand and to phase out nuclear energy and much fossil fuel use (including coal, because of possible associated environmental damage).

This chapter considers whether maintaining energy self-sufficiency up to 2020 by the means discussed earlier would be in the interests of more distant generations, and briefly examines the claims of proponents of low energy futures. We begin with some comments on the environmental effects of pursuing self-sufficiency, because one of the principal aims of low energy futures is to minimise such effects. Various policies are analysed initially without introducing discounting which we discuss in Chapter 9.

Environmental disruption

For both current and more distant generations, increased reliance on indigenous fuels up to 2020, by means of the policies discussed in earlier chapters, would raise energy-related environmental costs. Such costs are hard to quantify but they need to be taken into account in evaluating the advantages and disadvantages of such a policy. Clearly, imported energy avoids, for the United Kingdom, many of the external costs associated with energy production, so that increased indigenous production <u>per se</u> will most likely raise external costs. Changing the energy mix may well also raise external costs and have important implications for distant generations.

Even renewable energy sources such as wave, wind and tidal power, which may be relatively benign in terms of the global environment, are likely to be disruptive locally. Oil and gas operations in the North Sea appear relatively harmless to the natural environment (though not to those employed offshore). However, if operations move increasingly inland, countryside and community disruption may occur which imported supplies would have avoided. Coal mining involves costs in terms of health and safety hazards for miners and spoilt local environments, compared with importing coal, oil and gas. Coal burning also carries implications for current generations, especially in the supposed detrimental effects on forests and lakes that present processes impose[1]. Whilst the worst effects of UK coal burning may be felt in other countries, the costs are sooner or later likely to be borne by UK citizens since international agreements have as a basic principle that the 'polluter pays'[2]. Hence the UK might incur avoidance costs because it had to install expensive equipment which raised the cost of producing electricity from coal, or become liable for restitution to compensate for damage already done.

Although the thermal nuclear power programme relies on uranium imports, indigenous uranium deposits exist in parts of Cornwall, the Scottish Highlands and the Orkneys. Thermal nuclear power is also 'renewable' to the extent that spent fuel is reprocessed and used again. The degree of renewability is enhanced if the thermal programme is expanded to include fast reactors using plutonium from spent fuel originating in thermal reactors. More nuclear power stations, transportation of spent fuel, and reprocessing would involve increased routine radiation emissions and higher risks of accidents with major releases of radiation.

All of these additional costs current generations would need to compare with possible benefits before deciding whether, for them, the

pursuit of energy self-sufficiency would be
worthwhile. For more distant generations, the
major environmental concerns associated with the
types of self-sufficiency policies we have
described in previous chapters probably derive
from increased use of nuclear power and coal.
Current generations would bequeath their heirs an
economy more geared to the production and use of
nuclear power and coal than if policy had remained
unchanged. It may be that environmental problems
currently perceived to be associated with these
energy forms will be resolved, so that they come
to represent genuinely low-cost energy, taking
both internal and external costs into account. If
not, succeeding generations would have the option
of not using nuclear and coal plants, though that
would most likely be costly in terms of
restructuring the energy economy. Possibly,
however, in the future society might be _forced_ to
make such a costly restructuring if the
international community by then found the use of
coal and nuclear power unacceptable.

Perhaps a more important legacy than
additional nuclear and coal plants and greater
investment in nuclear and coal technology, is
possible increases in irreversible costs[3]
associated with nuclear and coal use, if Britain
pursues energy self-sufficiency. Radiation leaks
from nuclear power stations, reprocessing, or the
transportation of spent fuel could conceivably
damage present members of society, but they have
the choice, albeit imperfectly articulated through
the political system, of not opting for the risks
as well as the benefits of nuclear power. Future
members of society, who have no say in present
decisions, also risk suffering from a current
accident through genetic damage or ecological
disaster. Radioactive waste, whatever the storage
mechanism, carries with it some risk of failure
and some waste requires storing for hundreds of
years. Coal use also may impose irreversible
costs on distant generations not only in terms of
'acid rain' problems, but because it may be a main
contributor to the accumulation of CO_2 in the
atmosphere, which could produce climatic change
and threaten life support systems[4]. Future
generations thus bear some of the external costs
associated with coal and nuclear use in that
certain risks are imposed on them.

An intergenerational compensation scheme is
one way of solving the problem of shifting

irreversible costs onto future generations, who have no say in whether they accept or reject them. Compensation for future damages could, for instance, be from sums of money set aside to earn interest at the going market rate[5]. However, even assuming the political will exists to implement such a scheme, serious practical and moral problems would remain. The practical problems result from the difficulty of knowing how large the fund should be. The 'insurance' assessment would need to take into account the probability of the occurrence of an unfavourable event, such as a major accident at a nuclear power station, and the possible scale of damage, translated however imperfectly into money terms. For risk probabilities use is commonly made of available historical data on similar disasters which have occurred in the past. But for the kinds of events envisaged, there is little by way of past records from which objective assessments could be made, so that probabilities, however 'expertly' evaluated, would be largely subjective. Similarly, estimates of the size of the possible damage would need to take into account the timing, extent and duration of a potential disaster; they could be no more than educated guesses. Market interest rates would also have to be forecast over the lifetime of the compensation fund so that the size and timing of the necessary social contributions could be calculated.

The moral problem is essentially whether this kind of compensation scheme would adequately reflect society's attitude to risk and, in particular, to risks borne not by the generation taking the decision but by its successors. This point is discussed further in Chapter 9.

Resource depletion

To prolong self-sufficiency the United Kingdom would probably first postpone depletion (of oil) to eliminate the net export surplus. The 'banked' supplies would be brought back and further supplies of oil, gas and coal exploited to help forestall the importation of oil and gas that a 'policy unchanged' energy profile implies.

In the earlier chapters, we have adopted the same arbitrary time horizon (2020) as in the rest of the studies in this series. Extending self-sufficiency to 2020 may seem an act of self-denial

by today's society for the benefit of those who
live early in the twenty-first century. But what
of those who come later next century? Will they
regard a temporary extension of self-sufficiency
as neglectful of their interests? Viewed from
their perspective, such a temporary extension will
appear as accelerated depletion. Some finite
resources which could have been left for them will
have been consumed.

Whether finite energy resources would be of
greater value to society if they were left to be
exploited by later generations, rather than being
used to help maintain self-sufficiency for a short
period of time, is a virtually unanswerable
question, though it is helpful to identify the
variables relevant to the answer. The social
value of energy produced in any period equals all
the benefits (that is, the international market
price, representing the resource savings from not
importing, plus any extra social benefit not
passing through the market) minus all the costs of
exploitation (both internal and external). It is
probably reasonable to expect that the costs of
recovering the same reserves will fall over time
with technological advance; the external costs,
such as environmental pollution and community
disruption, may also fall. For example, mining
technology may well eventually allow underground
gasification of coal, allowing real extraction
costs to fall and reducing some externalities such
as damage to the landscape and loss of miners'
lives. Some of the reserves used to maintain
self-sufficiency, however, may come from enhanced
recovery from existing fields and mines. If these
reserves were instead closed in, it might be more
costly to recover them later. If, for the sake of
argument, we assume the costs of exploiting the
same reserves to remain roughly constant whenever
they are developed and produced, then the critical
variables are the international market price of
energy and any additional social benefit for the
UK attaching to indigenous supplies.

As far as the international price of energy
is concerned, no one - whether governments, other
market participants or energy 'experts' - can
predict the price of energy resources well into
next century. Nor is it at all clear what the
direction of change will be, since whether the
price rises or falls decades from now depends on
unknown demand and supply conditions. Although

world reserves of finite energy resources will
become absolutely more scarce between now and 2020
and beyond, only if available supplies are
perceived to be increasingly scarce relative to
demand is a rising trend in real price likely. On
the supply side, major new discoveries and
technological improvements could increase resource
availability; on the demand side, technological
change or changes in tastes could cut demand. For
instance, if alternative sources of energy from
the sun, hydrogen or the atom began to replace
non-renewables on a substantial scale, fossil
fuels and energy generally could become relatively
cheap worldwide. Alternatively, the energy market
might become more segmented because of limited
substitution possibilities. Fossil fuel might be
relatively expensive and limited to premium uses,
with other cheaper energy forms supplying the bulk
of society's energy requirements, being more
plentiful relative to demand. A gloomier
possibility is that major new discoveries of
finite energy are not made and technological
progress is slow. Then the world economy might
remain heavily dependent on fossil fuels and the
international price of traded energy could rise in
real terms over a long period. Whether it would
be more costly in terms of price to supplement or
replace indigenous energy by imported supplies in,
say, the early years of the next century or in the
second half of the century is entirely uncertain.
     Whilst acknowledging that, in the very long
run, it is unclear whether real energy prices will
rise or fall, society might wish to insure future
generations against certain possible outcomes, and
the preservation of finite energy reserves could
provide such insurance. Long-run price risks
might be perceived differently by private
companies as compared with society as a whole.
For the private company, unexpectedly low long-run
real prices may appear particularly damaging since
they would reduce profits or cause losses. Higher
than expected long-run prices would, ceteris
paribus, mean increased profitability.   For
society as a whole though, the worst possible
future outcome would not be that some undepleted
finite energy reserves became superceded by more
cheaply available energy, from home or abroad. A
more serious problem would be that, having
depleted to maintain self-sufficiency for a
limited period, the UK became heavily dependent on

expensive imported supplies. Unchanged policy or, better still, an even slower depletion profile would leave more finite energy resources available to cushion the worst effects of such an eventuality in the distant future. Energy self-sufficiency would ostensibly give total protection for a limited earlier period from the possibility of very high priced and economically damaging imported supplies (see Chapter 6). But adopting such a policy would, in effect, inflict on the UK immediately what it might be feared international energy scarcity would do sometime in the future - that is, significantly raise domestic energy costs and prices. Moreover, the creation of domestic monopolies would encourage higher than necessary costs and prices in the long run as well as in the short and medium terms.

Another social benefit that we suggested, in Chapter 5, might be attached to indigenous energy is a security of supply premium. Domestic supplies help protect the United Kingdom against damage from sudden disruption to imported supplies and lower the risk of threats to supplies and actual interruptions. However, just as aiming at lower UK energy costs and prices via a policy of self-sufficiency is likely to be self-defeating, so too is self-sufficiency unlikely to maximise security of supply. Even though it would protect the UK from sudden disruption to energy supplies from overseas, it would also increase the insecurity of indigenous sources. The security premium attaching to indigenous energy is thus greater when it supplies only a part of the UK's total needs than at self-sufficiency. Unchanged policy, or even slower depletion for oil and gas, would enhance security of supply for more distant generations in two ways. First, by providing a buffer against import insecurity and, second, by increasing the diversity of domestic sources, which would otherwise be concentrated in coal, nuclear power and renewables.

Energy self-sufficency to 2020 would provide few macro-economic benefits (Chapter 7) aside from the direct effects on the current account balance. Nevertheless, it would leave a legacy of step-change to society in later years, requiring faster and hence potentially more damaging structural change in the economy than would otherwise be required with slower depletion, especially of oil and gas reserves.

In general, as we have shown in earlier
chapters, adopting a depletion profile that helped
maintain UK energy self-sufficiency into the early
years of next century would be unlikely, during
the period of self-sufficiency, to produce either
lower energy costs and prices, increased security
from short-term disruption to supplies, or macro-
economic benefits compared with policy unchanged.
However, we have argued that to deplete finite
energy resources - especially of oil and gas -
more slowly than either self-sufficiency or
unchanged policy implies, could well be
beneficial. Such a policy is also capable of
conferring social benefits on more distant
generations by insuring them against:

- heavy reliance on very high-priced imports
  which might damage an economy still dependent
  on fossil fuels.
- interruptions to imported supplies.
- sudden structural change in the economy
  arising from a step-change to dependence on
  imports and renewables.

Renewable energy futures

It is an appealing thought that the UK could avoid
the energy and environmental problems of the
future by opting for environmentally benign and
indefinitely sustainable indigenous energy
supplies. Several research projects have looked
in detail at such possible low energy futures for
the United Kingdom[6]. They point to the imbalance
in government policy between cutting demand and
increasing supply, and the 'underfunding' of
research into renewable sources of supply compared
with the R & D spending on 'conventional' fuels
such as coal and, in particular, nuclear power.
In general though, analysis of these reports
suggests that, at best, a wholly renewable-
resource based economy is a very long way off.
Even then, it is infeasible, given present
population levels unless there are very drastic
changes in attitudes, lifestyles and economic
structures which all move in favour of such low
energy futures, including probably the widespread
acceptance of government coercion of consumers.

A recent such study[7], painstaking in its detailed analysis, presents four possible futures for UK energy consumption and production up to 2025. Two of the scenarios (Bl and B2) are 'conserver society' futures, based on low economic growth (1 per cent per annum to 2000 and 0 per cent between 2000-2025), the emergence of a 'post-industrial' economy with low energy intensity, and the development of 'environmentally aware' lifestyles and planning policies. The other two scenarios (Al and A2) are said to be 'technical fixes' which assume less qualitative change in the economy, individual and firms' attitudes and government policy, but rely more on rising material living standards and high economic growth (2.9 per cent per annum between 1976 and 2025) to effect change in energy use and supply.

All the scenarios nevertheless presuppose overwhelming government commitment to demand-side conservation and to phasing in of renewable energy sources. For example, all four scenarios present continuously falling energy consumption with total energy demand in 2025 ranging from 92 to 238 mtce, compared with our 'policy unchanged' range of 405-485 mtce in 2020, which already allows for considerable conservation in the future. Compared with our range for renewables (including hydro) on unchanged policy of 12-44 mtce in 2020, renewables contribute 44-110 mtce in 2025. Even assuming the enormous cut in energy demand which would almost certainly have to rely on government coercion, and the introduction of renewables on the scale envisaged (despite the likelihood of considerable local environmental and planning problems), renewable energy would still only account for between 26 per cent and 63 per cent of total forecast demand in 2025.

Nor will the high costs associated with a renewable energy future disappear once the 'transitional' phase is over. On present best estimates, renewable energy will continue to be high-cost and limited in availability. Security of supply could become a particular problem because of the regionally based nature of the supply system. Continual government vigilance to curtail demand on a long-term basis and intervention to prevent and alleviate short-term supply problems would therefore be necessary.

Whilst government-regulated demand is usually implied or explicitly called for to help implement and maintain low energy futures[8], it flies in the face of the conventional principle of demand, which is that consumers should be free to express their preferences in the market. Direct costs involved in bureaucratic rationing of energy would be considerable. But the indefinite need for government to define 'inferior uses' and decide who should get what energy and in which quantities, would be viewed by many people as an infringement of individual liberty and a very considerable cost. Moreover, conditions of low or zero material economic growth, which would probably be a prerequisite of renewable energy self-sufficiency, might not be generally perceived as the benefit many conservationists claim. They would oppose values presently held by the majority of citizens and jeopardise aspirations of higher living standards.

The implementation and maintenance of such an energy future would not be risk-free. Risks would include possible social and political unrest at home if costs associated with foregone economic growth (such as increased unemployment), government regulation of energy supply and demand, and coercion of the individual, came to be seen as excessive. Phasing out nuclear power and coal use by the UK would reduce environmental risks from these sources, but eliminating the possibility of global disaster originating from their use would require simultaneous and similar policy initiatives by all other user countries. Meanwhile, an economy which had shifted away from energy-intensive industries would nevertheless have to rely on energy-intensive imports. Hence the effects of unexpectedly high and economically damaging international energy prices would still be imported, albeit indirectly.

Energy self-sufficiency based on drastically cutting back demand, phasing out nuclear power, depleting oil, gas and coal slowly, and rapidly developing renewables would be very costly for present generations in terms of foregone consumption or alternative shorter-term, investment opportunities. Nor does it necessarily provide the most desirable or even the most sustainable energy future for more distant generations. Indeed, significant costs are likely to be attached to such a policy even in the long term. Any benefits derive from the assumptions that conventional fuels will become very scarce and expensive and that major environmental problems will continue to be associated with nuclear power

and coal use. Should these assumptions not hold,
then for distant generations the opportunity cost
of pursuing renewable energy self-sufficiency
would increase considerably.

Conclusions

All investment transfers consumption from present
to future and yields greater or lesser returns
over differing time spans. We have suggested that
investment to maintain self-sufficiency would reap
few, if any, net social benefits. However, energy
investment targeted to yield results further into
the future, to prolong a judicious mix between
imported and indigenous supplies and provide
diversified sources of domestic energy, could be a
valuable means of insurance for distant
generations.

If the United Kingdom was specifically
concerned to benefit more distant members of
society, the size and mix of investment in energy
would be somewhat different from that required if
self-sufficiency per se was pursued. Besides
encouraging some repletion of finite reserves by
enhanced recovery and the development of marginal
reserves, more oil, gas and coal would be kept in
the ground so that annual extraction levels were
below self-sufficiency. Research and development
would be concentrated on coping with the
irreversible costs at present perceived to be
associated with coal and nuclear power, and on
renewables. There would be an early and probably
somewhat larger policy shift towards encouraging
conservation rather than increasing supply. To a
certain extent, imports would be encouraged rather
than discouraged.

To calculate if it is worthwhile for the UK
to invest now to reap benefits for society far
into the future depends, however, not only on the
highly uncertain size of the net benefit, but also
on the valuation of the gains compared with later
or earlier gains. Whether and to what extent
later social gains should be valued less than
earlier benefits is a contentious issue,
especially when the costs may fall on one
generation and the gains on another.

Notes

1. Two recent publications on the 'acid rain' controversy are Energy Technology Support Unit, Acidity in the Environment, HMSO, London, June 1984 and Nature Conservancy Council, Acid Deposition and Its Implications for Nature Conservation in Britain, June 1984.

2. OECD, The Polluter Pays Principle, Paris, 1974.

3. For a more detailed discussion of irreversible costs see David Pearce, Ethics, Irreversibility, Future Generatons and the Social Rate of Discount, University of Aberdeen Discussion Paper 82-01, 1982.

4. See H. Flohn, Possible Climatic Consequences of a Man-Made Global Warming, International Institute for Applied Systems Analysis, Laxenberg, Vienna, (RR-80-30), 1980.

5. A.M. Freeman;, 'Equity, Efficiency and Discounting Intergenerational Effects', Futures, Vol. 9, pp. 375-6, 1977.

6. For instance, G. Leach et al., A Low Energy Strategy for the United Kingdom, the International Institute for Environment and Development, London, 1979 and Energy Technology Support Unit, Low Energy Futures, HMSO, London, 1982.

7. D. Oliver and H. Miall, Energy-Efficient Futures: Opening the Solar Option, Earth Resource Research Ltd, London, 1983.

8. In the Foreword to Energy-Efficient Futures it is stated that, 'In learning how to exploit renewables and how to use energy sensibly we lag behind other countries. If we continue with our present non-policy it is only too likely that in a few years we shall be buying know-how and ironmongery from Japan, the USA and the Continent. This will happen if we continue to fund at such a derisory level the development of ways of harnessing renewables, and depend on that nineteenth-century concept - the price mechanism - to bring about wise energy use' - (our emphasis).

Chapter Nine

EVALUATING ENERGY INVESTMENTS

Whether investment in energy, either to prolong
self-sufficiency into the early part of next
century or to benefit more distant generations, is
likely to be in the national interest depends not
only on the size and timing of potential benefits
and costs but also on the social discount rate.
That rate should ideally measure the opportunity
cost of not being able to use the resources
employed in the investment, either for current
consumption or to provide for the future with
different private or public investments. Some
form of discounting is always implicit in
decisions about the future. Even those who
believe they ignore discounting, in effect use a
zero discount rate and therefore make an implied
judgement about present versus future use of
resources. The extent of discounting is, of
course, particularly important in contemplating
very long-run investments.

In this chapter we look briefly at the
difficulties of choosing social discount rates,
making allowance for risk and uncertainty, and at
how British governments have tried to resolve
these difficulties. We then consider more
explicitly what rates would be appropriate for the
evaluation of energy investment designed to
prolong self-sufficiency or benefit more distant
generations.

Capital markets in theory

Despite long and wide-ranging academic argument,
there is as yet no consensus on how to select
appropriate social discount rates[1]. The leading

contenders are some direct estimate of 'social time preference', representing society's preference at a given time for a small increase in current welfare over a similar increase some time in the future, or alternatively an estimate of the opportunity cost of using the resources for public rather than private investment. The problem is to obtain such estimates.

If capital markets operated perfectly, there would be no conflict between time preference and opportunity cost of capital measures of the discount rate and the appropriate rate would be observable in the market. In the perfect markets of the theorists, the assumptions of perfect knowledge and costless exchange ensure that all social costs and benefits are incorporated in market transactions and eliminate the uncertainty of the future. Society then exchanges present consumption for future consumption until the marginal social time preference rate (the sum of individual time preference rates) in any period equals the marginal rate of return on the 'investment' of postponed consumption. Since investment is expected to be productive, a given total of postponed consumption should result in larger consumption in the future, but market equilibrium rates of interest are such that the average member of society is indifferent between investing or consuming marginal income.

Producers in such markets carry out investment projects so long as the expected rate of return exceeds the rate of return required by investors. Thus, with each individual saving to the point where his or her marginal rate of time preference equals the relevant rate of interest, and with real investment carried by producers to the point where its marginal productivity also equals the rate of interest, no conflict arises between society's 'time preference' and 'productivity' or 'opportunity cost of capital' rates for discounting either private or public investment. A government then simply uses the same discount rate to test whether proposed public investments are likely to be in the national interest as private companies use to test the profitability of similar private investment (allowing for differences due to taxation).

Changes in equilibrium interest rates occur with changes in society's time preference rates or in production possibilities. In an ideal situation, they ensure a continuous reassessment of the best allocation of society's resources between present consumption and saving, between private and public investment and between different projects in each sector. Perfect capital markets would therefore provide a flexible structure within which the necessary reassessments for efficient resource allocation could take place.

No actual market works like the theoretical ideal, but the theory of perfectly functioning markets and of market imperfection and failure provides a useful benchmark against which to compare the working of imperfect real-world financial markets. We discuss below how comparisons between real and ideal markets affect the approach to discount rate choice for evaluating investment to prolong self-sufficiency and to benefit more distant generations. Whilst market rates can probably be taken as a basis for determining the former, 'free-rider' problems may render market information of little value as an index of very long-term social time preference rates.

Social discount rates and energy self-sufficiency

Under-saving may be a problem in real-world markets because imperfections cause saving and investment to be less than the public 'really' wishes to undertake. Under-saving may occur, for example, because of restricted outlets for private saving or because information is lacking about saving opportunities. In these circumstances, governments acting in the national interest would adopt either market-improving policies - such as increasing saving outlets and spreading information - or a market-displacing strategy. The latter would involve raising funds by taxation and using them to increase public investment and stimulate private investment so long as the return on either exceeded 'true' social time preference rates. Since the purpose of the exercise would be to increase the total volume of saving and investment compared with the market outcome (rather than to shift investment from the private to the public sector), it would not be sufficient for the government to operate through the (imperfect) market and simply increase borrowing.

In practice, it is unlikely that in the UK, where the financial system is well developed, individuals are forced into higher than desired levels of current consumption because of financial market imperfections. Saving for the sake of distant generations may well represent a special case, as we discuss in a later section. But we need not be unduly concerned that, because of market imperfections, governments should force society to save more (by increasing taxation or cutting public spending) in order to invest to prolong self-sufficiency.

We can therefore reasonably assume that, in evaluating investment to prolong energy self-sufficiency, the resources used would be withdrawn from some other potential investment in the public or private sector. If we have an idea of the return that foregone investment could have achieved over the same period, such a figure can be used as the social discount rate to test whether energy self-sufficiency is worthwhile. The government adopts this opportunity cost of capital approach in its guidelines to nationalised industry investment (see below), but those guidelines are not entirely appropriate for our purposes since cost and benefit flows from different prospective investments need to be comparable.

There may, for instance, be significant external costs associated with a project which mean that an apparently high private return represents only a low social return. Projects can generate external benefits as well as external costs but, whilst private producers will be anxious to ensure that consumers pay for all the benefits of private investment, they have little incentive to ensure that all social costs (such as environmental or community disruption) are internalised. Similarly, there is no particular reason why many public bodies (such as the nationalised industries) should of their own volition internalise external costs. Since we have tried to take into account non-marketed social costs and benefits when evaluating energy self-sufficiency, it would not be appropriate to compare a small social return on that investment with a higher private or internal return on a foregone project. However, the extent of any adjustment is virtually impossible to estimate.

If under-saving is not a problem, and if public investment could be assumed risk-free, one way to estimate the social discount rate would be to use the government's long-term borrowing rate

Evaluating energy investments

as a proxy for the social time preference rate. That rate should approximate also the opportunity cost of capital for public projects. Two difficulties, however, arise with this approach. The first is that rates of return on government securities reflect short-term influences arising, for instance, from the operation of monetary policy, which are not relevant to society's long-term social discount rate. Second, a guaranteed return on government 'gilt-edged' investment does not mean that public investment is risk-free. If governments consistently underestimate the financial riskiness of public undertakings, the risk will be carried by taxpayers and not investors in government bonds, and there is no reason to believe that taxpayers are any more risk-loving than private investors.

Social time preference rates and distant generations

Economists are sometimes criticised for assuming that individuals in their economic transactions are selfish or self-interested[2], dominated by concern with personal and family welfare and indifferent to the welfare of others. It is not true, however, that altruism – in the sense of concern for the welfare of more socially distant and unknown members of society – is absent from capital or other markets. Each individual is free to save or consume according to his or her preferences, whether they are selfish or non-selfish, and social time preference rates in the market will accordingly register the degree of altruism revealed by such individual behaviour. But unless it is assumed that individuals are perfectly altruistic, valuing the welfare of all equally with their own, then a 'free-rider' problem is likely to exist in a large community.

Assume that some individuals are altruistic to a degree, in that they wish to benefit (say) distant generations, but that they value personal and family welfare more highly. Then such people will be happy to leave other altruists to provide for the distant members of society, since they consider only their own negligible contribution to the fund of saving in deciding whether or not to 'free-ride'. It is possible that, by reasoning about the unfortunate outcome if everyone behaved

in the same way, individuals might decide to
co-operate spontaneously and the market solution
would be preserved. Some writers[3] have indeed
expressed a belief in a 'contagion' theory such
that, if members of society act 'as if' altruistic
in one area of life, then by example the same kind
of 'as if' behaviour will spread to other areas.
Similarly, it has been suggested that a diminution
of the opportunity for altruism in one area, for
instance by changing the system of blood
donation[4], would weaken a general tendency to
spontaneous altruistic behaviour in the
community. But the welfare of distant generations
has no particular emotional appeal to raise
people's consciousness (as for instance details of
the plight of children waiting for blood
transfusions or kidney transplants may do).

The possibility of 'as if' behaviour apart,
there does appear to be good reason to think that
individual saving for the sake of distant
generations will be below the socially optimum
level. If that is so, then the government can
legitimately increase taxation and invest to
benefit distant generations, though it is clearly
very hard to calculate how far it should go. We
might, in theory, look to the political decision-
making process for the answer, and assume that
through that process individuals express their
willingness to be taxed for financing very
long-term investment that they collectively
desire. But just as real-world markets are
imperfect, so too are democratic processes[5]. The
British political system, for instance, may place
parties in power with only minority electoral
support. Furthermore, electors vote for a package
of policies and projects and not on individual
issues. Consequently there is little relation
between taxation and the stream of benefits
received from specific public investments.

If there is no way of properly summing
individual preferences to give a 'true' social
time preference rate for distant generations, we
might ask if there is any a priori reason for
supposing society would choose to give much or
little weight to the welfare of distant
generations. Such an overall social time
preference rate would implicitly include two types
of discounting. The first discounts utility —
that is, quite independently of future levels of
real income, the same unit of welfare may be
considered to be worth less in the future than in

the present. It is usually held that individuals discount for social distance[6] much as they discount their own future welfare due to impatience or myopia. Thus one would expect society's 'utility' discount rate as applied to the welfare of distant generations to be positive. (By contrast, pure altruism would ensure that the welfare of distant generations was valued equally with society's present consumption and would indicate a zero discount rate for utility.) Gains in welfare accruing to future generations will also be discounted due to real income growth, in much the same way as individuals would take account of their own future real income levels in a personal time preference rate. Therefore, if distant generations are expected to be richer per capita than society is now, the 'income' discount rate will also be positive. In other words, if it is generally expected that society will continue to increase its living standards, little weight will be attached to distant welfare. If it is believed that society will suffer deprivation in the future, for instance because of resource or environmental limitations or population growth, then the overall social time preference rate may be zero or even negative. Thus, as with other social time preference rates, the 'appropriate' rate for discounting very long-term investments will incorporate both value judgements and empirical assessments about the future. Nobody can say with any degree of certainty therefore what the 'proper' rate should be, and individuals and groups in society will have differing opinions about it.

One way of overcoming such disagreement is to disregard individual views and have the government impose what it regards as an appropriate rate for evaluating very long-term investment. Alternatively, individuals or groups may attempt by moral persuasion, and by claiming superior knowledge of future events, to promote a social consensus as to the correct weight to be attached to the welfare of future generations. Economists have been amongst those who have suggested that present generations should consider whether the outcome of summing subjective preferences would be 'fair' as far as distant generations are concerned. Perhaps the most famous comment along these lines is Ramsey's in the introduction to his model of optimal saving - 'We do not discount later enjoyments in comparison with earlier ones, a practice which is ethically indefensible and arises merely from the weakness of the imagination.'[7] It was to try to ensure that such ethical judgements are detached from day-to-day decisions that Adam Smith invented the 'impartial spectator'. More recently Rawls[8] advocated that such decisions be taken as if by a hypothetical assembly of random representatives from each generation ignorant of their own positions within society.

By the process of persuasion and moral criticism, individual preferences can and do alter. The 'environmental movement', for example, which is concerned essentially with the long-run impact of man's activities on the natural environment, has undoubtedly had a significant effect on the views and behaviour of individuals in both their market and political roles. Moral persuasion is an accepted and important influence on society's preferences. But those who seek to persuade others to adopt a particular attitude to distant social welfare, need to be able to claim not only moral superiority but also more accurate views of the future.

If society is forced by governments to save substantially more resources than it would freely choose, for the sake of increasing the welfare of distant generations, then costs will immediately be felt in the form of undesired lower current living standards and curtailment of individual liberty. This would lead to a questioning of the basic assumptions underlying such a policy and, in a democracy, the eventual dismissal of the government. If, however, governments choose a long-term social discount rate that is higher than society (if fully informed) would have chosen, there is much less chance of a public outcry. By definition, no obvious costs would be felt by present members of society, and therefore there is no incentive to question the assumptions underlying the policy choices; the social costs would be reaped by our successors.

We must express some doubts, therefore, whether real-world governments have much incentive to apply low discount rates to prospective very long-term investment, when the costs will fall on present voters and the benefits depend so much on judgement about society's living standards decades or centuries from now. Since the primary aim of politicians is to gain or re-gain office, there is likely to be an overriding emphasis on the short-term effects of decisions. In areas of public policy which are likely to be of little overall consequence, and where decisions are easily reversible, such a short-term emphasis may be unimportant. But present-day energy policy may have a considerable impact on society in the long term and the consequence of some policy decisions may be irreversible. In these circumstances, politically shortened time horizons might have very unfortunate side-effects on future generations.

We would conclude that it is virtually impossible to decide on a 'correct' rate for discounting very long-term investments, and difficult to decide even on the relevant range within which one might expect the correct social rate to lie. Anyone evaluating very long-term investments therefore has to make a judgement, as we have done at the end of this chapter.

Risk and uncertainty

A problem common to evaluating investment to prolong energy self-sufficiency and investment to benefit distant generations is to make adequate allowance for risk and uncertainty. Risk and uncertainty have two components - the future outcome, and the probability that each possible outcome will occur. The word 'risk' is usually reserved for situations where a history of similar situations exists, so that an objective probability distribution can be attached. Pure uncertainty is then used to describe situations where no such history exists, so that at best only a personal subjective probability distribution can be attached. Most situations mix objective and subjective inputs so that real life is characterised neither by pure risk nor by pure uncertainty[9].

Two issues are particularly relevant to this study:

- how to account for the extra health and environmental risks to present and future generations associated with additional coal-fired and nuclear power stations which would probably form part of a policy to prolong energy self-sufficiency to 2020, and how emerging energy technologies should be assessed from the point of view of physical risk;

- how to allow for the very considerable
uncertainty surrounding resource cost and
benefit flows from very long-term energy
investment - a problem which applies, in
probably less extreme form, to investment to
prolong self-sufficiency.

In considering these issues, we divide the
discussion of risk and uncertainty into two
categories, one covering physical risk and the
other dealing with monetary flows, though in
practice the two are inter-related.

Monetary flows: Whilst individual attitudes to
uncertainty vary with the risk-taker, most savers
are generally held to be risk-averse and will
demand a higher expected return as compensation
for uncertainty. If an investment could be
undertaken as part of a large pool, so that very
little risk attached to the average returns per
project in the total pool, or if the risks
attached to single or multiple projects could be
spread across many investors, then the risk
premium attaching to individual projects could be
very low. If the risk-pooling and spreading was
very wide, then individual investment projects
could possibly be treated as if their outcomes
were certain, and could be judged by their net
present values unadjusted for risk.

It is on this kind of argument that public
investment is sometimes said to be risk-free or
low-risk, whilst a criticism of real-world capital
markets is that they fail to provide sufficient
opportunity for pooling claims to uncertain future
returns, and thus generate higher discount rates
than socially desirable. With risks presumed
pooled in the public sector, the appropriate
discount rate to use for public investment is
therefore apparently lower than for comparable
private sector appraisal.

A particular problem often singled out to
prevent perfect risk-sharing in the market is the
existence of 'moral hazard', by which is meant the
possibility that a person or company might buy a
claim contingent upon the occurrence of a certain
state of affairs and then try to influence events
to bring it about. High policing costs may
therefore be necessary to prevent moral hazard, in
turn impeding the establishment and efficient
operation of markets. Incomplete and costly
risk-pooling would be the result. A more

difficult and commonplace problem for markets to cope with is uncertainty. 'True' risk can be insured against, albeit imperfectly, but when particular types of investments have not been repeated in large enough numbers to enable an objective probability distribution to be attached to the uncertain costs and returns, market transactions will be severely hampered by lack of information.

If market devices for overcoming risk and uncertainty are imperfect, and investors are inclined to risk-aversion, the likelihood is that some projects will not be adopted in the private sector even though their expected return is positive. The argument seems persuasive, however, that the sophisticated financial markets in the UK and elsewhere ensure quite effective pooling of statistically clear 'risk', upon which governments would find it hard to improve, while uncertainty is as difficult for governments to cope with as markets. But the belief that single government projects can be treated as 'risk-free' could encourage a tendency to public sector 'risk-loving', where projects are undertaken whose expected return is negative. Once under way, the pressure of interested parties, problems associated with foreclosing, and the difficulty of effective monitoring by the adminstrators responsible, can ensure continual investment of taxpayers' money in projects which are most unlikely to result in net benefits to society.

It is difficult to decide what is the best way to incorporate adequate allowance for the risk and uncertainty surrounding future cost and benefit flows in public project appraisal. A risk premium is sometimes used to take account of the normally higher rate of return required on a risky investment. However, this approach is not much favoured because a uniform premium does not take proper account of the expected timing of the uncertainty, and biases investment against capital-intensive and long-run projects; furthermore, the difficulty remains of assessing the size of the premium. Another approach is to carry out a sensitivity analysis, and present expected cost and benefit flows in terms of ranges, showing how the return changes with different assumptions about key variables. Sensitivity analysis is, of course, highly subjective and can easily be manipulated to suit the analyst or decision-maker.

The incorporation of risk and uncertainty in public project and policy appraisal is undoubtedly problematic. Nevertheless, there seems to be little reason to suggest, as a general rule, that less allowance needs to be made for risk and uncertainty in the public sector than in the private sector. Since risk and uncertainty are not generally welcomed by society and are costly to cope with, it does not seem a particularly good idea for governments to encourage risk-taking. Therefore the uncertainty surrounding possible net benefits from prolonging self-sufficiency should not be played down by virtue of pooling arguments.

A somewhat different attitude might legitimately be adopted towards basic energy research. For private firms and their shareholders, doubts about whether to invest in ventures which will yield net benefits only in the very long run, if at all, are compounded by uncertainty as to whether they will be able to capture all the fruits of their own invention. For society, on the other hand, production and then widespread distribution of knowledge are highly desirable. Therefore a case can be made for undertaking public investment in energy research and development (or encouraging private investment) on a less cautious basis than private firms would adopt.

Physical Risk : The government cannot eliminate risks to human life and the environment by pooling or spreading. In theory, those members of society (present or future) who assume such risks could be compensated, and the government could attempt to ameliorate the effects of the event should it occur. However, limited knowledge makes it very difficult to estimate the extent of adequate compensation for carrying risk associated with energy technologies, and the size of any emergency fund.

Observation suggests that acceptance of risk depends in part on whether participation is voluntary or involuntary. For acceptance of risks which are beyond the control of the individual (involuntary risks), higher compensation seems to be required. Moreover, there appears to be less public concern about the possibility of a number of widely distributed small-scale accidents than about the possibility of major catastrophes. Thus, 'experts' may assess nuclear power as low-risk, because of the low probability of occurrence of a major disaster and the comparative safety in day-to-day operations; at the same time, they may define solar power as high-risk because large numbers of solar panels are required per unit of energy and these require considerable amounts of steel, glass and other components, the manufacture of which generates physical risks.[10] The general public, however, appear to rank nuclear power as high-risk[11], not because they necessarily disagree with expert probabilities (which cannot be other than 'expertly' subjective), but in particular because if, say, a major accident occurred, large numbers of people would be affected at the same time, and because the risk is seen as beyond individual control. Deaths or injuries involved in the production of energy from solar panels will, by contrast, be spread through time, and offering oneself for employment in any of the industries concerned would probably be deemed a voluntary risk. Thus what 'experts' deem low risk, the ordinary member of society may consider high risk and vice versa.

It may be possible to reduce the 'lay' social risk, or to convert it into a more acceptable form by changing product design. This could reduce the size of a possible catastrophe or its probability, or convert a risk from involuntary to voluntary (for instance, a change could be made to smaller safer power stations sanctioned by referendum). Alternatively, if society's very risk-averse attitude to catastrophes and involuntary risk was changed, the social costs of 'risky' investments such as nuclear power would be reduced. Some people have attempted to point out that laymen's present attitudes to differing risks are 'illogical', in an attempt to lower the risk-aversion to nuclear power[12]. If coal-burning becomes 'singled out' as a major public issue in the same way as nuclear power has been, then the same contradiction between lay and expert analysis of the attached social risks will probably occur.

Dislike of involuntary risk might logically make present generations even more risk-averse towards the prospect of future generations carrying environmental and physical risk from present-day activities than they are to carrying such risks themselves, since distant generations have no direct say in whether or not they participate in such risk-bearing. Certainly individuals who express great concern for the welfare of future generations are likely to define 'fair' attitudes to future physical and environmental risks as 'more cautious than we would apply to ourselves'.

The size of the social costs associated with physical and environmental risks will thus vary with both preferences and empirical estimates of the effects. Some groups in society attempt to lower the social costs by persuasion, whereas others try to raise them by the same method. The size of risks, and hence costs, governed by empirical estimates of damage, will also vary depending on who is composing the figures and interpreting the results. Nevertheless, the ranges of estimates from different sides should narrow with improved availability of data.

For the purpose of this study, the imposition of extra 'physical' risk on present and future generations must in itself be counted as an extra social cost to be set against possible benefits from a self-sufficiency policy, together with any extra provision necessary to cope with a resultant environmental or health-related emergency. Allowance for involuntary risk-bearing by future generations would probably need to be higher than allowance for similar risk-bearing by present generations.

The overall size of the additional costs is very difficult to estimate since, strictly speaking, one is dealing with uncertainty rather than objective risk. Probably the best that could be done in a detailed cost/benefit analysis, would be to conduct a sensitivity analysis to show how the overall result would respond to changes in key assumptions about discount rates, benefits and costs. But even then the limits of the range for environmental hazard would necessarily be very wide, since the size of such costs is likely to be particularly volatile through time, with fluctuating preferences and newly emerging data. Costs falling at different times would need to be incorporated at the appropriate social discount rate. Costs to distant generations, for instance, should be included at the appropriate long-term rate. A positive long-term rate would diminish such distant costs in present value terms, but a negative rate would enlarge them.

As far as investment in new energy technologies is concerned, perceptions of risk and uncertainty should be borne in mind. Many people appear to find uncertainty about possible dangers more unacceptable than a clearly-defined risk which is evidently of similar size. Sometimes it has been suggested that a cut-off date should be used in investment evaluation when very long-term, potentially large but very uncertain costs or benefits are present. But this would have the same effect as using a high positive discount rate to cope with risk and uncertainty in project appraisal, which also effectively shortens the time horizon. Both methods, in effect, make costs and benefits after a certain date 'disappear'.

Government policy[13]

UK government official policy towards social discount rates and allowance for risk and uncertainty is contained in three White Papers published in 1961, 1967 and 1978[14], which attempt to clarify the economic and financial objectives of nationalised industries, since the nationalisation statutes were couched in terms too vague to give operational guidance.

The 1961 White Paper gave no explicit advice on project evaluation, but emphasised that one of the purposes of the financial targets then set for the nationalised industries was to ensure that they did not account for a share of national investment which could not be justified by prospective returns. In other words, it used an 'opportunity cost of capital' approach to public investment appraisal.

The 1967 White Paper was more explicit and instructed nationalised industries to appraise investment projects using a test discount rate (TDR) of 8 per cent in real terms, raised to 10 per cent in 1969. The test discount rate attempted to measure the marginal opportunity cost of capital to the public sector, and was decided after a survey of large firms to discover the ex-ante real rate of return sought by them on marginal low-risk investment projects. Though the attempt to specify a marginal social discount rate in this way was later officially abandoned, the opportunity-cost rationale, dominant in official thinking even in 1961, has remained so ever since.

With a whole-hearted application of the approach, all investment yielding a positive net present value when discounted at the relevant discount rate would be undertaken. If, for some reason, the government wanted to control the total of public investment for a period (apply 'capital rationing'), then the relevant marginal opportunity cost would not be the return on a comparable private investment but the return on the last-accepted public investment. What happened in practice, however, was that when governments wanted to cut public investment for a time, cuts were made across the board irrespective of prospective returns.

The framework of economic rules and guidelines outlined in the 1967 White Paper was only ever implemented half-heartedly. Use of the test discount rate, probably the easiest part of the guidelines to enforce since investment programmes had to be vetted by sponsoring departments, was very partial. Large parts of investment programmes were categorised as 'necessary' or 'replacement' and not evaluated. Thus the test discount rate had little effect on the overall scale of public investment, which was decided through administrative and political processes informed by macro-economic considerations, and not by the acceptance of all projects which passed the TDR (as efficient resource allocation would have suggested). Allocation between different public projects depended on political priorities and the competing bids of the agencies and their bargaining positions. The major application of the test discount rate was to certain (not all) cost-minimising exercises, such as the choice between a nuclear and coal-fired power station.

The 1967 White Paper made only limited reference to how risk and uncertainty should be handled in investment appraisal. It recommended the assessment of a likely range of outcomes and that higher risk projects should be assessed using a higher test discount rate. This, as noted earlier, is a traditional way of handling risk, but is only appropriate if the risk is directly related to the timing of the cash flows, otherwise it will bias the investment decision against long-lived and capital-intensive projects.

Although it was never formally withdrawn, the set of rules established in the pursuit of efficient allocation of resources between public and private sectors and between public investment projects by the 1967 White Paper was demoted in the preoccupation of the late 1960s and 1970s with macro-economic ends (particularly the control of inflation). In 1978 the government published another White Paper setting out a revised system of economic and financial control, an innovation in which was the introduction of the Required Rate of Return (RRR) criterion. This was set at 5 per cent in real terms and has not been altered since. Nationalised industries are required to achieve 5 per cent ex post on new investment programmes as a whole,though it is not clear what check there is on their achievements. Each industry can in theory choose its own discount rate for project appraisal, the 5 per cent RRR being an average required return based mainly on a survey of pre-tax real rates of return achieved on assets by private companies in the mid-1970s. Whilst 5 per cent was not stipulated as a test discount rate, it has in fact been used as such, for instance to evaluate the proposed Sizewell 'B' nuclear power station and in official studies of the potential for renewable energy sources; 5 per cent would appear to be, de facto, the official test discount rate for most purposes.

The 1978 White Paper left the problem of allowing for risk and uncertainty unresolved, and simply noted that the nationalised industries should discuss allowance for risk and for 'appraisal optimism' with their sponsoring departments. It also stated, in re-establishing financial targets played down in the 1967 White Paper, that the financial targets would not depend only on consideration of resource allocation, but also upon the weight given to social and wider economic policies, such as the need to counter inflation.

The conceptual and practical problems of measuring social time preference rates are cited in Appendix 1 of the 1978 White Paper. However, the focus on the opportunity cost of capital is retained. Estimates of the cost of capital to the private sector and estimates of the social time preference rate are used as a rough cross-check on the 'reasonableness' of the actual RRR figure of 5 per cent.

Policy conclusions

The function of the social discount rate is simultaneously to determine the optimal volume of total investment in the economy, the optimal split of that total between public and private sectors, and the best allocation of total public investment between projects. The rationale is that, to maximise social welfare, the expected marginal rate of return on new investment should be equal to the social time preference rate. Otherwise, welfare could be increased by re-allocating resources between consumption and saving, and investment funds between sectors and projects.

If under-saving is likely to be a problem because of market imperfections, or if markets seem likely to fail accurately to record society's intentions (for instance, towards distant generations), then in theory governments intent on maximising welfare should intervene. Their objective would be to ensure that both private and public investment is carried out so long as the expected return exceeds the true social time preference rate, though the estimation of such a rate is extremely difficult.

The philosophy of the 'opportunity cost of capital' approach to social discounting takes as given the total level of investment in the economy, and seeks to optimise the split between private and public investment and different public projects. On this basis, the test discount rate for public policy appraisal should therefore be a forward-looking measure of marginal opportunity cost.

Opinions differ on the extent to which uncertainty surrounding expected costs and benefits should be taken into account in public project and policy appraisal, but a theoretically risk-neutral approach to total public investment may well translate in practice into a policy that takes too little heed of the riskiness of specific projects. This could be particularly so in the case of physical risks which are involuntary and potentially catastrophic, to which society seems particularly risk-averse.

Governments have generally adopted an opportunity-cost approach to public investment, and the test discount rate set in 1967 was meant to be a forward-looking measure of expected marginal returns in the private sector. By contrast, the required rate of return criterion introduced in 1978, and so far unchanged, was a backward-looking measure of achieved average returns in the private sector, applied to a nationalised industry's investment programme as a whole rather than to individual projects. It has since been used as a forward-looking marginal opportunity cost of capital measure. In practice, the partial use of the test discount rate, the difficulty of enforcing the RRR system, and government's preoccupation with short-term macro-economic management rather than long-term efficient resource allocation, make it unlikely that systematic public policy appraisal and implementation will occur.

As regards investment to prolong self-sufficiency into the early years of next century, there seems no reason to dispute the government's opportunity-cost approach to social discounting, since market under-saving need only be a serious consideration as far as more distant generations are concerned. In the absence of information on expected returns, the social discount rate has to be assessed on the basis of achieved returns. For our purposes, the government's rate of 5 per cent may be on the high side since there may be a bias in both private and nationalised industry investment towards projects with net external costs. Also, rates of return on (non-oil) private sector investments in the UK have declined a little since the RRR was set in 1979. Nevertheless, since we have suggested that if there are any net benefits from pursuing self-sufficiency they would be minor, even a lower rate would ensure a negative net present value.

The uncertainty surrounding possible net benefits from pursuing energy self-sufficiency should not be lightly dismissed, since society's resources might well be wasted as a result. A policy to prolong self-sufficiency that relied on considerably increasing nuclear and coal use might underestimate the social costs, and hence social opposition, to implementation of the policy; official and lay thinking still appear far apart on how the risks from such energy sources should be measured and perceived. Nor can one expect much enthusiasm for the rapid introduction of new energy technologies where the costs - both environmental and resource costs - are still so uncertain, and the benefits are perhaps even more uncertain, depending on the non-availability of reasonably priced imports.

Because energy investments - oil and gas, coal and nuclear, renewables and conservation - are presently discounted at very varying rates, there is probably a case in theory for some government intervention to bring the rates in line. The aim would be to ensure that all energy investment is discounted at the social rate, and that cost and benefit flows are comparable. The effect would probably be some deferral of oil and gas production and more investment in conservation and repletion measures, but there is no logical reason why energy self-sufficiency should be the result. The outcome might instead be a socially judicious mix between domestic and imported supplies.

Markets will probably under-provide for distant generations. The problem of free-riding suggests under-saving, and the considerable uncertainty surrounding very long-term research and development, especially involving the benefit flows as far as private companies are concerned, will inhibit potentially socially advantageous investment. The government therefore needs to be involved in taxing and encouraging investment in very long-term projects. What discount-rate ranges should be used for evaluating such projects, and hence the extent of saving, depends on empirical estimates of long-run social welfare levels as well as the degree of altruism in society towards future generations. A low (or negative) discount rate would imply an altruistic attitude towards distant members of society, or a cautious (pessimistic) assumption about living standards in the distant future. Such a rate would be consistent with the idea, put forward in the previous chapter, that society might wish to insure distant generations against particularly harmful possible future eventualities. Therefore we consider a lower rate is probably justified for evaluating very long-term investment than for investment to prolong energy self-sufficiency. Nevertheless, if taken to extremes, cautious concern for distant generations could involve heavy sacrifices by present generations for the sake of those in the future who may, in the event, be much better-off. Whatever the very long-term social discount rate, it should be used for all such investments rather than being partially applied as seems to be the current practice. For instance, fusion research and research into renewable energy technologies seem not to be evaluated on the same basis. Present social attitudes to physical and environmental risks associated with energy systems do, however, suggest that society might be particularly risk-averse as far as possible irreversible costs falling on distant generations are concerned.

Lower very long-term social discount rates would considerably bias energy policy in favour of slower depletion of UK oil, gas and coal reserves, more investment to recover now marginal reserves, and increased investment in energy conservation. Greater physical risk-aversion on behalf of future generations would bias policy against investment to build more nuclear and coal-fired power stations on the basis of present designs, and encourage investment in evaluating and overcoming environmental problems associated with these energy forms. Lower social discount rates would also encourage more investment in research and development into new demand- and supply-side energy technologies, though society's cautious attitude to environmental risk would need to be as fully incorporated as possible in the project evaluations. The overall result would still be a judicious mix of indigenous and imported energy supplies, but the definition of what was judicious would change.

1.   For a discussion and additional references see David Pearce, Cost Benefit Analysis, Macmillan, London, second edition, 1983.

2.   See David Collard, Altruism and Economy, Martin Robertson, Oxford, 1978.

3.   Ibid., chapter 16.

4.   R.M. Titmuss, The Gift Relationship, Allen & Unwin, London, 1970.

5.   The Economics of Politics, Institute of Economic Affairs, London, 1978.

6.   M. Olson and M. Bailey, 'Positive Time Preference', Journal of Political Economy, Vol. 89, No. 1, 1981, pp. 1-25.

7.   F. Ramsey, 'A Mathematical Theory of Saving', Economic Journal, Vol. 38, (December 1928), pp. 543-59.

8.   J. Rawls, A Theory of Justice, Harvard University Press, Harvard, 1971.

9.   For a general discussion of risk and numerous references, see Peter G. Moore, The Business of Risk, Cambridge University Press, Cambridge, 1983.   For discussion of risk and uncertainty in project appraisal see David Pearce, Cost Benefit Analysis, op.cit.

10.   See H. Inhaber, 'The risk of producing energy', Proceedings of the Royal Society of London A, 376, 1981, pp. 121-8.

11.   P.   Slovic,   B.   Fischhoff,   S. Lichtenstein, 'Fact versus fears: understanding perceived risk', in   R. Schwing and W.A. Albers (eds.), Societal Risk Assessment: How Safe is Safe Enough?, Plenum Publishing, New York, 1980.

12.   Lord Rothschild, Risk, The Dimbleby Lecture of the British Broadcasting Corporation, London, 1977.

13.   See David Heald, 'The Economic and Financial Control of UK Nationalised Industries', Economic Journal, June 1980.

14.   The Financial and Economic Obligations of the Nationalised Industries, Cmnd., 1337, HMSO, London, 1961; Nationalised Industries: A Review of Economic and Financial Objectives, Cmnd., 3437, HMSO, London, 1967; The Nationalised Industries, Cmnd., 7131, HMSO, London, 1978.

Chapter Ten

SUMMARY AND CONCLUSIONS

The history of energy self-sufficiency

In the period between the two World Wars, when the
United Kingdom was still a large-scale producer
and exporter of coal, the country had a
substantial (though diminishing) export surplus of
energy (Table 1.1). After the rundown of the coal
industry during the Second World War, however, the
UK became a small net energy importer and its
import dependence grew to about 50 per cent by
1973, the year of the first oil shock (Table 1.2).
Postwar British governments showed varying
degrees of interest in energy self-sufficiency as
a policy aim. For a few years after the 1939-45
War, when home-produced coal was the country's
dominant source of fuel and its output was
recovering from its depressed wartime level, it
seemed that home energy supplies might be
sufficient to meet the greater part of demand.
But political interest in self-sufficiency faded
from the late 1950s onwards: by then the British
coal industry had resumed its decline because of
competition from low-priced, imported oil.
Governments concentrated instead on tempering the
effects of fuel market forces on coal and other
indigenous energy suppliers by giving them a
degree of protection from oil.
Then, in the 1970s, interest in self-
sufficiency was resurrected, mainly for two
reasons. First, because rising oil prices and the
very uncertain world oil market led most countries
to try to reduce oil import-dependence. The
second factor was more specific to Britain.
Discovery of substantial oil reserves in the early
1970s transformed Britain into one of the world's
major oil-producing countries. The UK'S swift

move from 50 per cent energy import dependence in
1973 to a 20 per cent export surplus ten years
later (Table 1.2) was primarily a consequence of
the rapid growth of offshore oil production. Over
that period energy output rose by 202 mtce, of
which oil contributed 194 mtce (Table 1.2);
production of offshore gas and of nuclear
electricity increased by much smaller absolute
amounts, and coal output continued to decline
gradually. The UK's energy self-sufficiency ratio
of about 1.19 in 1983 was higher than in 1938
(1.1) but lower than in the early 1920s (1.35)
when coal exports were still very large (Table
1.1).

Now that energy self-sufficiency has been
attained, and indeed exceeded, a question which
arises is whether governments should take
deliberate action to extend the period of self-
sufficiency. Much of this book is devoted to
discussing various policy issues which arise in
trying to answer that question.

The future, on unchanged policy

To establish a base point, we consider in Chapter
3 how energy self-sufficiency might change up to
our time horizon of 2020 if government policy
remained unaltered. The estimates are necessarily
very uncertain, but the production and consumption
ranges we use suggest that, for a number of years
yet, UK energy production will remain sufficiently
high relative to home energy consumption for
self-sufficiency to appear a feasible policy aim.
It appears to us likely (though by no means
certain) that, on our unchanged policy assumption,
the energy self-sufficiency ratio would fall below
one in the 1990s (table 3.1). Nevertheless, for
much of the period 2000-2020, UK fuel production
would probably be significantly higher relative to
consumption than it was in the 1960s and early
1970s; on our optimistic assumptions Britain would
still be close to energy self-sufficiency around
the year 2000. In such circumstances it might
appear self-evident that governments should aim to
change policies so as to extend self-sufficiency
in energy. It would not be surprising if there
were pressures on governments, from indigenous
energy producers and others, to institute an
explicit energy self-sufficiency policy.

Summary and conclusions

Policy approaches

There are three main avenues of approach to such a
policy, as we explain in Chapter 4. The first is
output deferral. Starting from a net export
position, as does Britain, some energy output (in
practice, mainly oil) could be deferred to a later
period when there would otherwise have been net
energy imports. Thus self-sufficiency would be
prolonged by a policy of changing the time-
distribution of output. In practice, such a
policy might lead to many costs and complications
which would offset potential benefits. For
instance, the oil companies' willingness to invest
would diminish because the expected net present
value of their oil reserves would most likely
decline, and they would require incentives if a
reduction in total oil recovery from the North Sea
was not to occur; governments would find
'fine-tuning' of production and consumption
extremely difficult; and the oil market would
probably become highly politicised so that
resources were diverted from efforts to improve
efficiency to lobbying.

A second approach to self-sufficiency is by
means of 'repletion' to increase the total amount
of energy produced in the United Kingdom in a
certain period. Accelerating depletion rates
could be used as a temporary expedient. But more
important would be measures which increased the
quantity of energy eventually produced in the
United Kingdom. Governments could, for example,
encourage enhanced recovery from fossil fuel
reserves which would in any case have been
exploited and production from reserves which
otherwise would not have been developed at all.
More investment in nuclear power and renewables
could also form part of a repletion programme.
Governments would need to take two kinds of action
to encourage repletion: some enabling measures
(such as more liberal licensing procedures) would
probably be required, and steps would have to be
taken to increase the attractiveness of energy
production both to nationalised industries and to
private companies (for instance, by reducing
taxes, increasing subsidies or raising prices).
The costs of repletion would arise from
the investment of resources in the necessary
measures from increased external (for example,
environmental) costs and from the more politicised
energy market which would probably result from
greater government involvement in decision-making.

138

The third approach to self-sufficiency is by demand-side conservation. Governments would attempt to bring about lower energy use, at any given level of output in the economy, by such means as consumption taxes, subsidies for energy-saving, and possibly by rationing energy supplies. The costs of a conservation programme would be similar in nature to those incurred in production deferral and repletion measures, and in addition there might be some government coercion of consumers.

The three approaches to a self-sufficiency policy have one feature in common: each involves 'over-investing' in the sense of channelling more investment in a particular direction than if government policy remained unchanged. Such additional investment implies that society incurs costs by aiming at self-sufficiency, since the resources could have been used elsewhere; and there may be extra costs associated with increased government control of the energy market. Thus, when one considers whether a self-sufficiency policy is likely to be socially beneficial (rather than merely feasible), expected benefits have to be set against these expected costs, both discounted at the appropriate social discount rate. It may, for instance, be that there are hidden social benefits of indigenous energy production which, in effect, mean that the international market price of such energy is below its social value. Indigenous production would then be less than socially optimal and demand would be greater than the optimum. Or the government may be able to correct market imperfections such as the use by private companies of 'excessive' discount rates which lead to under-investment.

Security of supply

One possible social benefit of being self-sufficient in energy is increased security of supply. Our discussion of this subject in Chapter 5, however, concludes that a self-sufficiency policy is more likely to reduce than to increase the security of Britain's energy supplies. An explicit government commitment to maintain self-sufficiency means that a greater proportion

of energy supplies is indigenous, so that the
consequences of indigenous supply interruptions
are more serious. The probability of
interruptions (or threatened interruptions) is
also likely to increase because of the greater
leverage which indigenous producers obtain when
they are given enhanced monopoly power by the
government. It is highly significant that the one
fuel for which British governments have pursued a
policy close to energy self-sufficiency is coal:
imports have been strictly controlled when they
showed signs of becoming troublesome, and exports
have in recent times generally been small relative
to output so that the British market has been
supplied essentially from British mines. It seems
probable that the frequent threats to disrupt
supplies and the three serious interruptions which
have actually occurred since the early 1970s (see
Chapter 2) have largely stemmed from the
considerable bargaining power which a de facto
self-sufficiency policy has given the British coal
industry.

Our discussion of security of supply suggests
also that the costs of emergency provision against
indigenous supply loss are likely to be increased
by a policy which largely excludes energy
imports. Nor is it possible for Britain to
insulate itself from the effects of international
energy market crises by pursuing self-
sufficiency. The only real benefit which self-
sufficiency would be likely to bring is avoidance
of the immediate, direct effects of an energy
embargo specifically aimed at UK imports.

In general, a self-sufficiency policy pursued
in order to gain extra security of supply would be
futile, though there might for a time be some
increase in perceived security. Society would
incur the costs of the policy but would most
likely find its real security reduced because it
would lose the diversification of supply sources
which foreign trade brings. Nevertheless, some
'over-investment' to promote security of supply
may be justified, since there might be under-
provision by private markets. Consequently, there
is a case in principle for some output deferral,
repletion and conservation(as there is for some
government investment in energy storage). The
policy would aim not at self-sufficiency but at
maintaining a judicious balance between imports
and home supplies (and diversified sources of
each) well into the future. In practice, there

would be many difficulties in the way of determining how much extra investment there should be and, in particular, of avoiding excessive monopoly power accruing to indigenous producers.

Price-related benefits

After Britain's comparatively short period of energy export surplus, a self-sufficiency policy would reduce net energy imports and would tend to increase prices. Although there are several ways in which a country pursuing a self-sufficiency policy might eventually hope to achieve benefits in terms of lower energy costs and prices, we conclude in Chapter 6 that such a policy in the UK would be unlikely to realise net benefits.

Britain is not a large enough country in world energy trade to have any significant long-term influence on international prices by pursuing self-sufficiency. Even if it were, so long as the country remained self-sufficient it could obtain little direct benefit from lower prices abroad. So any gains from self-sufficiency would have to result from lowering the costs of indigenous supplies. A possible gain could come from a temporary period of self-sufficiency in which Britain's energy industries realised economies of scale, invested in the latest technological advances, and generally lowered costs. We are, however, very sceptical whether such 'infant industry' type protection is appropriate for Britain's major fuel suppliers. There would be little incentive to improve efficiency during the period of protection and, in practice, it would prove extremely difficult to bring that period to an end. It is all too likely that long-run costs and prices would be increased, not diminished.

There is a case for government support for some basic research in the energy industries on 'public good' grounds, and for indigenous energy sources which offer the prospect of being environmentally benign and low-cost in the long term. But such assistance for energy resources which may become important in the long run is not to be justified on self-sufficiency grounds per se. It is much more a matter of promoting a judicious mix of supplies so as to keep down prices by maintaining competition between fuels.

141

Summary and conclusions

It may also be argued that indigenous energy supplies are particularly valuable since, in the long run, there may be unexpected and damaging increases in imported energy prices, so that apparently high-cost indigenous supplies may turn out to be relatively low-cost. This argument has some substance but its logical conclusion is not that self-sufficiency should be the objective. Aiming at self-sufficiency for this reason would involve forcing on society immediately costs which might otherwise occur well into the future (if at all). Provided society is willing to bear the cost, it may be worth paying some insurance premium in the form of higher energy prices to guard against the worst effects of such price increases later. Assessment of the size of the 'correct' premium would be very difficult, but it would be remarkable if the optimal solution was to aim at self-sufficiency.

If one could assume that a self-sufficiency policy would be implemented by an omniscient, altruistic government, it might be reasonable to anticipate some price-related gains. Such a government would control the monopolistic tendencies and inefficiencies which seem to us an inevitable accompaniment of any policy which excludes or greatly diminishes competition from foreign supplies. In the real world, however, it is very unlikely that governments would be able effectively to suppress monopolistic forces; indeed, experience suggests they might identify with producers and act against the interests of consumers.

Macro-economic effects

In discussing macro-economic effects of self-sufficiency (Chapter 7), we consider two periods - the 'deferral period' in which output is initially held back and then increased (compared with a 'policy unchanged' production profile), and a subsequent repletion period in which the main aim of policy is to increase energy output. In both periods, there might also be demand-side conservation.

During the deferral period, since energy output would initially be lower than with unchanged policy, there might be some small adverse effects on real GDP, government oil tax revenues, employment and the balance of payments, compensated by favourable effects later. The impact of deferral on the exchange rate - probably initially reducing it and later increasing it - would tend to even out these effects.

A degree of output deferral might be justified on macro-economic grounds in that it would smooth out the decline in oil output which is probable from the mid-1980s onwards. A benevolent and far-sighted government would wish to avoid sharp oil-production-induced variations in the exchange rate and in oil tax revenues, the consequent need to shift resources between industries, and the effect on inflation of sudden changes in costs. The government might therefore regulate production so as to achieve a smooth transition for Britain from net energy exporter to net importer. It might also use other measures, such as gradual introduction of a tariff on crude oil imports or increasing taxes on oil products consumed in the UK, so as to replace lost revenue and promote conservation. Output regulation would, however, be difficult in practice and we have doubts whether governments would actually be willing to defer production; if they did, they would in effect be handing over macro-economic benefits to future administrations. But, whatever one thinks of the case for deferral, there seem to us no grounds for deferring output to <u>prolong self-sufficiency</u>. Such a policy could only result eventually in a sharp drop in production (unless a repletion policy was already in being), bringing the need for rapid economic adjustment as the exchange rate fell and oil revenues declined abruptly.

Once output deferral was no longer capable of maintaining self-sufficiency, the economy would enter what we call the repletion period, in which self-sufficiency could be sustained only if government policies resulted in the production of energy which would otherwise have been judged unprofitable. We see some scope for carefully-judged repletion measures to bring macro-economic benefits (for instance, to real GDP, employment and the balance of payments through the employment of otherwise unused resources), but it seems highly improbable that governments should replete to the extent of self-sufficiency. If they did, significant gains from international trade would most likely be relinquished and the policy would probably lead to the kind of monopolised and

Summary and conclusions

politicised energy market discussed earlier. The
problem of 're-entry' would also be accentuated
once repletion was no longer able to sustain
self-sufficiency and indigenous energy output fell
sharply. Another effect would probably be to
re-distribute income away from consumers towards
indigenous energy producers (as the producers'
bargaining strength increased), with some
regressive effects because of the low income
elasticity of demand for energy.

Distant generations

Extending self-sufficiency into the early part of
next century by output deferral and repletion may
seem like an act of self-denial by today's society
for the benefit of people living thirty or forty
years from now. More distant generations,
however, may see such a temporary extension of
self-sufficiency as accelerated depletion: some
finite resources which they could have used will
have been consumed. In addition, they could
suffer from irreversible environmental effects of
actions taken long before their time by energy
producers, consumers and governments.

In Chapter 8 we argue that it is virtually
impossible to know whether finite energy resources
would be of greater value to distant generations
than they would be to the generations who come
before our time horizon of 2020. How the social
value and the social costs of energy will change
by (say) the later years of next century is so
uncertain that there seems little we can
contribute except to criticise the naive view that
energy is bound to become more expensive in real
terms. In the face of such uncertainty, however,
it is possible that society might wish to insure
distant generations against some of the dangers
they could face. A temporary self-sufficiency
policy would be inappropriate, but there is a case
for preserving finite energy resources as such a
means of insurance, by deliberately depleting
those resources more slowly than the market
would. In effect, such a policy would aim to
maintain far into the future the judicious balance
between imports and home supplies which we have
already recommended.

We also examine briefly whether distant
generations would benefit from a move to much
greater reliance on renewable energy sources. Our

conclusion is that extensive government coercion
would probably be necessary if renewables were to
achieve a high share of energy consumption in the
foreseeable future; drastic measures to cut demand
and then hold it down would be required and
material living standards might well decline.
Security of supply might be reduced by greater
regionalisation of the energy system. Moreover,
it is only if non-renewables become very expensive
in the long run, or continue to suffer from major
environmental externalities, that distant
generations are likely to gain from a policy of
'over-promoting' renewables.

Evaluating energy investments

Chapter 9 discusses some of the difficult issues
surrounding choice of a social discount rate. The
5 per cent rate in general use in the UK for
public projects may be on the high side.
Nevertheless, even if a lower positive rate was
used, it would not affect our conclusion that
extending self-sufficiency into the early years of
next century would not be worthwhile since we
argue that social benefits (before discounting)
are unlikely to be significant. We foresee
problems in implementing a policy of prolonging
self-sufficiency by increased use of coal and
nuclear power because of perceived health and
environmental risks. We suggest also that there
is unlikely to be widespread support for a policy
of drastically cutting energy consumption and
introducing new supply technologies rapidly.
There is a case for ensuring that rates of
discount are similar for different energy
investments. If that were so, there would
probably be some deferral of oil and gas
production and more investment in conservation and
repletion; however, such action has no logical
connection with pursuing self-sufficiency.

There may be a tendency to under-saving in
the sense that markets may under-provide for
distant generations. Thus there may be a case for
some government encouragement for very long-run
energy research and development (for instance,
using a relatively low discount-rate range for all
such investments) though not for self-sufficiency
reasons. The discount rates used in evaluating
such investments should reflect the degree of
social concern for distant generations and how

well-off they are expected to be. Society is likely to be particularly averse to imposing irreversible costs on distant generations. If discount rates for evaluating very long-run investments were to be reduced (compared with those used at present), energy policy would be biased in favour of slower depletion of non-renewable resources, repletion and conservation. Risk-aversion might shift policy away from investment in nuclear and coal power stations and towards investment in evaluating the environmental problems perceived to be associated with these forms of energy.

General conclusions

Our overall view of self-sufficiency policy is that it would undoubtedly bring costs to society and that significant benefits are very unlikely to accrue. Some of the 'benefits' which self-sufficiency advocates evidently foresee seem to us more likely to turn out as costs; in particular, it seems quite probable that a self-sufficiency policy in Britain would lead to a market characterised by reduced security of supply and higher-cost energy.

Although our contention is that a self-sufficiency policy would be a crude and costly instrument, we would certainly not suggest that there are no opportunities for government to improve on the outcome of energy markets. Those markets, after all, contain numerous imperfections and fail in various ways. Thus it should be possible for far-sighted and benevolent decision-makers to pursue market-improving strategies to the advantage of society as a whole. For example, we have suggested that there might be social gains from some production deferral and a measure of repletion. The idea would be to compare the expected marginal social costs of such action with the expected marginal social benefits (difficult though that comparison would be) in deciding to what extent to defer and replete: the aim would be to maintain a judicious mix of diversified imports and diversified home supplies well into the future. That would be quite a different matter from adopting the arbitrary target of maintaining self-sufficiency.

Unfortunately, as we point out at various places in the book, in recommending action by government for the sake of society as a whole one encounters the fundamental difficulty that political systems are not perfect. Knowledge of present and future preferences and of future events is imperfect so that governments are unsure what actions would benefit society. Even assuming that the long-run social interest could be identified, electoral systems do not give politicians the incentives to follow policies which might be in that interest. Thus politicians - and probably also Treasury civil servants - are unlikely to be receptive, for example, to arguments that oil production should, in the long-run national interest, be deferred. They are more likely to respond to pressure from the producers for repletion, which may thus be carried too far.

There seem to be essentially two ways in which such problems can be remedied. The first is constitutional and political reform aimed at improving the representativeness and responsiveness of government - or, in economists' language, reducing the imperfections of the political market place. We leave it to political scientists to comment on such matters. But the second remedy lies more in the hands of economists, among others. It is to point out the underlying issues in debates such as that on self-sufficiency, placing them on the political agenda in the hope that, though there are no clear answers to the difficult questions which arise, explicit analysis will be helpful.